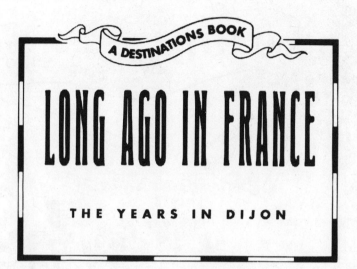

A DESTINATIONS BOOK

LONG AGO IN FRANCE

THE YEARS IN DIJON

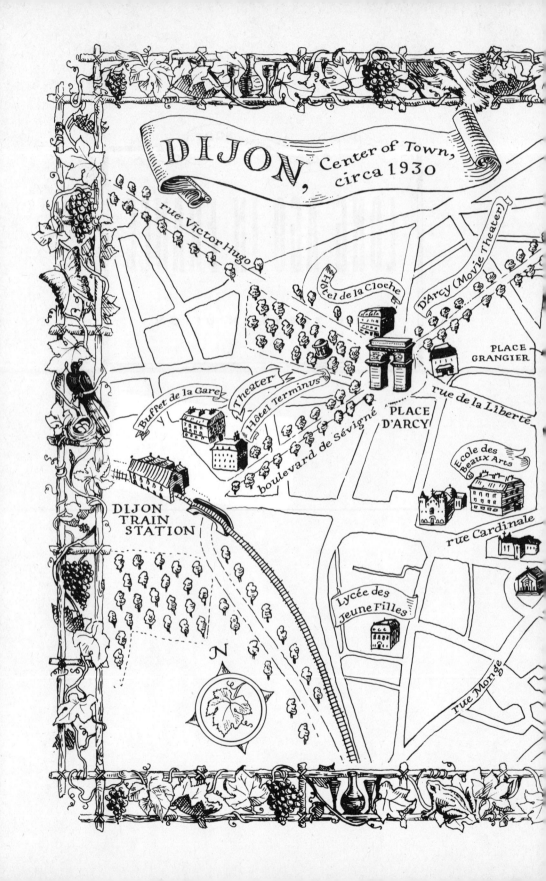

DIJON, Center of Town, circa 1930

rue Victor Hugo

Hôtel de la Cloche

D'Arcy (Movie Theater)

PLACE GRANGIER

Buffet de la Gare

Theater

Hôtel Terminus

rue de la Liberté

PLACE D'ARCY

boulevard de Sévigné

École des Beaux Arts

DIJON TRAIN STATION

rue Cardinale

Lycée des Jeune Filles

N

rue Monge

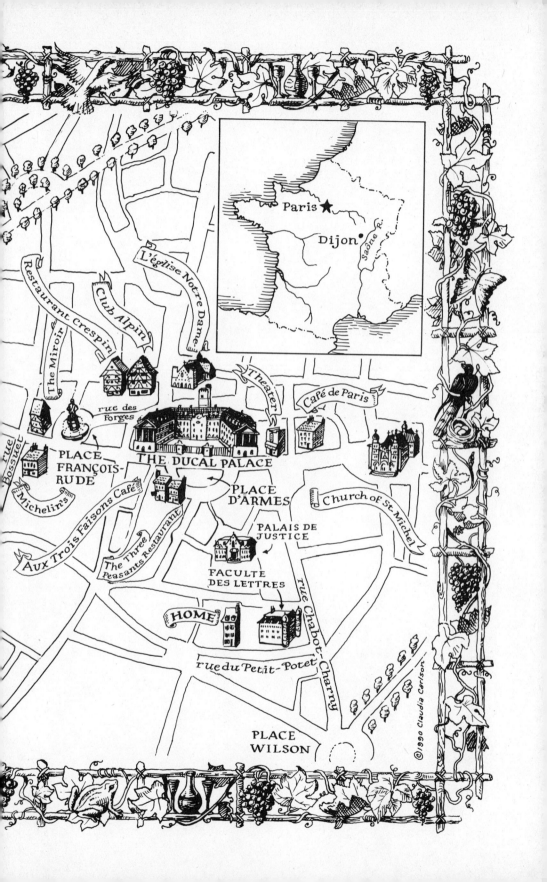

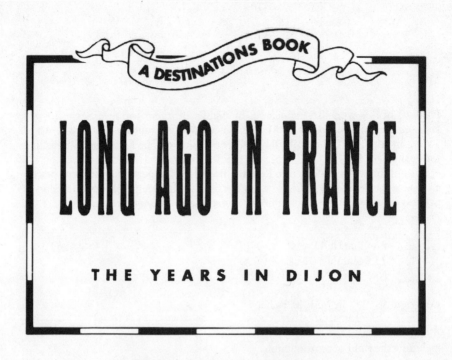

A DESTINATIONS BOOK

LONG AGO IN FRANCE

THE YEARS IN DIJON

M. F. K. FISHER

INTRODUCTION BY JAN MORRIS

PRENTICE
HALL
PRESS

NEW YORK   LONDON   TORONTO   SYDNEY   TOKYO   SINGAPORE

Portions of this work first appeared, in slightly different form, in *Serve it Forth* and *The Gastronomical Me* by M. F. K. Fisher and are reprinted from *The Art of Eating* by M. F. K. Fisher with the kind permission of The Macmillan Publishing Company.

The author is also indebted to Perigree Books for the permission to reprint several excerpts from *With Bold Knife & Fork,* and to Kathleen Hill for permission to use several excerpts from an unpublished manuscript, *Conversations with M. F. K. Fisher.*

 Prentice Hall Press
15 Columbus Circle
New York, New York 10023

PRENTICE HALL PRESS and colophons are registered
trademarks of Simon & Schuster, Inc.

Library of Congress Cataloging-in-Publication Data
Fisher, M. F. K. (Mary Frances Kennedy), 1908–
    Long ago in France : the years in Dijon / M.F.K. Fisher.
       p.   cm.

    1. Fisher, M. F. K. (Mary Frances Kennedy), 1908–   . 2. Food
writers—United States—Biography.   3. Dijon (France)—Social life
and customs.   I. Title.
TX649.F5A3   1991
641'.092—dc20
[B]   90-23071
                                                                                                   CIP

Designed by Robert Bull Design

Manufactured in the United States of America

CONTENTS

INTRODUCTION

by Jan Morris

It was a lucky day for the world—I do not exaggerate—when in the year 1929 the young American M. F. K. Fisher arrived in the French city of Dijon. She was new to Europe, new to France, new to marriage, and, not least, new to cookery. Dijon made her. It put her on the road to a unique position in twentieth century letters. She is far more than merely one of the world's most celebrated writers on food, and the author of two previous and famous books about France. She is the possessor of an unmistakeable and universally admired literary personality that has given her a status all her own. W. H. Auden said that nobody in America wrote better prose. John Updike once called her "a poet of the appetites."

It was fortunate too that she and her husband happened to choose this particular French city for postgraduate study. Dijon is one of those grand old middle-size cities of France that seem largely impervious to fashion. The ancient capital of Burgundy, it stands at the head of its vineyards somewhat complacently, I always think, far enough from Paris, well away from the frenzied Rhone valley, even managing to ignore the great highways that scuttle through its purlieus. If you wanted to choose a city to illustrate generic France, so to speak, you could do much worse than Dijon.

One can imagine how powerful its impact must have been upon a sensitive young American woman sixty years ago. In *Long Ago In France* Mrs. Fisher recalls, with an intimacy that is always self-amused, her growing up in the old city. She learns to speak French there. She learns to understand French ways and prejudices. She tries her hand at the journal, the essay, and the short story. The marvels of the French cuisine are gradually revealed to her and she begins to sense (one reads between the lines) the first traumas of marriage. The threads of her later life are spinning themselves already, and it is not fanciful to say that in the streets, cafés, and dining rooms of this city the Fisher way of writing is in genesis.

It might be thought that such an essay in recollection would be a period piece, and in some ways of course it is. Not only is its author a little older now (and is sometimes drawing, as her aficionados will recognize, upon material already published), but the city she describes, the society she recreates with such affectionate detail, has matured too. A war has happened to France since then, and technology has altered the French as it has altered all of us. The prospect of a united Europe has shifted French perceptions. Universal travel has brought the rest of the world nearer. Old cities like Dijon, self-assured for centuries, can no longer be quite so sufficient to themselves, so like city-states. Even the French cuisine has had its ups and downs, or more properly its ins and outs, since the young M. F. K. Fisher first tried the *diner de luxe au prix fixe* at the sign of the Three Pheasants.

Besides, she is writing about herself in youth. When she later went to live in Aix-en-Provence and Marseille, she looked at those cities through the eyes of an experienced woman, a gourmet and a stylist. In Dijon she was just a girl, learning as she went along. The experiences she records in these pages are untrameled by comparison, just as Dijon itself in those days was less like other cities. We are dealing here with the sensibilities of a young American of the 1920s, interacting with the personality of a between-the-wars city of France.

And yet in another sense the book is not a period piece at all. Times have certainly changed in Europe, but I think nearly every reader will find that Mrs. Fisher's responses to France in 1929 are astonishingly like our own six decades later, so that we easily recognize all her emotions, and feel ourselves sharing her attitudes. Restaurants have come and gone, lodging-houses have been demolished, the characters of Dijon, I dare say, are not quite so picaresque as they used to be. Yet upon the foreigner that old charmer of a country still exerts the same fascination, does it not? We still feel freer there, somehow. The people seem, rightly or wrongly, just as variously original. The food is mostly still marvellous. Sitting in a café doing nothing is just as much fun.

Even as I write this, though, I wonder if I am telling the truth. Have I just been bewitched by the book, so that its responses have magically overlaid my own? Has time been confused in my mind? Is it all literary illusion? Perhaps, but then all art is illusion, and a *genre* of art was born when the young M. F. K. Fisher knocked on her first door in Dijon long ago, looking for somewhere to live.

PREFACE

This book will prove that I have always been a reporter and perhaps a writer, because it is made of complete sentences in my head, some of which I have put down and some of which are still buzzing about there inside. This is one reason why it is often hard for me to remember whether they have already been written and where.

It seems that I have kept a diary or a journal or have written short stories all my life; and, although they were not printed until I was well into my twenties, phrases and whole sentences from them are as clear to me now as when they were written, if indeed they were. I find them in unexpected places . . . stuck in my mind as well as in a cupboard or a forgotten box of old letters, and it is impossible for me to know what has been published, or indeed what has ever been said by me aloud.

When I first went to Dijon to live with my husband, Alfred Young Fisher, I kept at least two journals going and wrote often of dreams and other experiences in the third person. Sometimes these were published later, and even now they turn up in whole journals or in forgotten letters that I never posted. I know that there are many people I must thank for letting me repeat, consciously or not, what I may have said to them or written to them or even for them, to be reprinted in magazines and journals. I hope that I do not offend anyone by printing here in this account of my first three years of life in Dijon things that have already been said or written by me.

It was there, I now understand, that I started to grow up, to study, to make love, to eat and drink, to be me and not what I was expected to be. It was there that I learned it is blessed to receive, as well as that every human being, no matter how base, is worthy of my respect and even my envy because he knows something that I may never be old or wise or kind or tender enough to know.

I shall forgo all the pleasant preliminaries, the neat little essays and even whole books about getting to Dijon. I have said it before, more than once, and printed it too: yes, I was married for the first time in Southern California, on September 5, 1929; and yes, it was good to be there in France less than two weeks later, and in love. I admit to it all.

So . . . on about September 20, I left my husband on the steps of the Faculté des Lettres on the rue Chabot-Charny in Dijon, France, and went bravely and alone into the dank, dark, horrible old building. Al and I parted almost happily, knowing that we would be alone and together from that fine minute on, forever and forever. We were in love, and so full of that special bliss that I forgot that I could neither speak nor understand the only language that everyone there spoke as if he had always done so, which was indeed the case.

I managed somehow to pull out enough of the new language to get a list of boardinghouses for foreign students. This was such a heady experience that I actually enrolled myself in what was called the Cours des Vacances, with a shy, round, pink-cheeked little man, whom I soon came to know as Monsieur le Professeur Martenot, an important faculty member. Then I walked up through the strange streets which from that instant on were never strange to me again, because I had become a ghost forever.

I honestly don't know how I managed to walk so jauntily away from Monsieur Martenot's dingy office, and then find my way like a homing pigeon or an angel-guided idiot through the crooked narrow streets that led me to exactly where I should have gone. But there I was, standing in the center of the place d'Armes, which was in the center of Dijon, and therefore in the center of France itself. In other words, the whole world was mine. (And it stayed that way for as long as I lived there in that strange ancient city . . . and in fact it still is the center, for me and for most of the time . . .)

It seemed quite natural then that hot afternoon to stroll across the large half-moon of the fine old parade-grounds that face the monumental façade of the Ducal Palace, then to step up to the rows of *fiacres* that still waited always there for passengers. I had never ridden in one, although only two or three nights before I had listened to the clear sounds of a couple of them clip-clopping along the quay underneath our windows in Paris, and I had recognized their sound without question as part of the reality of the dream I was to live in from then on.

I stepped up to a waiting *fiacre* that had a little brown cotton canopy to shade me. The coachman was plainly drunk, and the old horse wore a straw hat, with gloves crocheted from thin red string for his ears sticking out of the crown. I roused the old man enough to show him the printed address Monsieur Martenot had put in my hand, and we set off slowly, what with the September heat and the gentle booziness of the *fiacre* driver. It all seemed quite natural, as indeed it was.

Once off the rue de la Liberté, though, we picked up a definitely jaunty speed as we turned right, and headed for the second time that afternoon down the rue Chabot-Charny, and then we turned smartly if somewhat unsteadily to the right again, just beyond the shabby *faculté,* and headed straight for the meanest-looking house on the little rue du Petit-Potet. Like all other residential streets in the town, it presented a continuous blank face of high façades pierced by the big closed arches of the doorways and shuttered windows. We pulled up with what seemed a special flourish in front of the correct number and the driver said, *"Et voici,"* in a loud voice before he sagged back in a sudden alcoholic snooze. I climbed down from the woven straw-covered seat and onto the uneven cobbles as if drawn to that number, and crossed the narrow sidewalk.

The house was two stories tall, with four shuttered windows on the second floor, and there was a large barred window on either side of a big arch on the ground floor, which looked tightly covered by wooden doors. I felt alone and scared but still full of the elation of having met and been able to talk with a citizen of this ancient place.

Then I found that a very little door had been cut in the big dark wooden doorway that filled the arch. I knocked firmly on it with an air of finality and excitement that indeed has never left me. And I know now that my new life as a ghost started there, when it opened and I stepped over the sill and into the courtyard.

CHAPTER

ONE

OMEONE SHRIEKED harshly to come in. Madame Ollangnier darted from the kitchen, which lay just beyond the dining room, under the first rise of the staircase. She had on a filthy apron, and I could hear someone rattling pans and chopping and beating.

It was a real Burgundian town house, in two parts, one on the street and the other at the back of a deep narrow courtyard. The entrance to the whole place was, of course, the little door cut in the great double door that once had let carriages into the courtyard. Immediately to the left, there was a door into a room that probably had been an office, which I soon found out was a *salle de bains* but was never used as a bath. It was filled with baskets and old trash, a regular mess of a room.

On that same side, facing the courtyard, although I did not see it until later, was an almost cozy latrine, and to my right in the long cave formed by the second story of the house were two doors which at one time may have been the concierge's lodgings, but which now housed the dining room and kitchen for the whole house. There, the landlady told me, we would eat well, three times a day, with her husband, her stepson, one or two carefully selected students, and herself.

At the far end of the forlorn courtyard was what would be called the main part of the house of three stories. On the bottom floor were four beautiful tall French doors, then on the second floor there were four windows, and on the third floor, where we would soon be living, there were only two smaller windows.

On the ground floor, with two steps up to tall French windows, was the office of Monsieur Ollangnier, who was the official town architect. We soon learned that he went out often into the country appraising old *châteaux* and monuments, declaring them unfit for public use or too rare to walk in.

The next three French doors opened into the *grand salon* of the house, which was the temporary but beautiful bedroom of Madame Bitsch, the central figure in the one picture hanging in the dining room, and the very ancient mother of Madame Ollangnier. She was a real heroine as I was soon to learn: a member of the Legion of Honor. She had been a great leader in the defense of Dijon during the Franco-Prussian War when the Germans invaded. Madame Bitsch was from Alsace, and she had come down to Dijon ahead of the Germans and got all of the housewives into the streets with ironing boards and chairs to make great barricades to stop the Germans. Then they climbed on top of the piles and shook their brooms at the invaders, who turned back unable to fire on the fierce women. So the women saved the town of Dijon from the Germans in 1871, and Madame Bitsch *was* a great heroine!

While we were there, Monsieur Ollangnier tried, for about the tenth time, to get her the Lavender Rosette, but, unfortunately, he never succeeded.

In the picture she was a strong big woman up on top of a huge barricade made of beds and chairs and kitchen tables, and she was saying: "Lead on! Lead on!" *"Allons les Enfants!"* She looked like a glorified La France, with her wild eyes and her hair flying.

When we were there Madame Bitsch was a tiny little old old woman, and I do not think we ever met her officially. We used to peek at her when we came home from the theater or from carousing around at night, as we climbed the great stairway to our rooms on the third floor. She would always be sitting up straight in a beautiful old bed with great white puffy pillows and a white coverlet, with a red satin puff at the bottom. She wore a white nightgown, up to her neck and down to her wrists, and a little red shawl around her shoulders, and a little red nightcap. She was quaint, fascinating. She was very romantic.

She started to die every once in a while. She was a chore for Madame Ollangnier, and it was the joke all over town that Madame Bitsch had had more last sacraments read over her than any other woman in the town, because Madame would joyfully call the priest and say, "Mother's dying! Mother's dying!!" and he would give her Extreme Unction, and then she would revive.

I do not know if that story was true, but I know that Madame really loved her. She cared for her like a precious jewel, in spite of having to take care of the mostly bedridden old lady.

On the second floor of the house at the back of the courtyard (they called it the first floor; we would call it the second) there was indeed a drawing room; a little drawing room, with a big piano in it, because Madame Ollangnier was a musician. There was the bedroom of Monsieur and Madame; above was the third floor, where we were to stay. On the side of the courtyard that was not just a plain wall facing the Archbishop's garden, a covered stairway zigzagged up the side, connecting the two halves of the house, floor by floor.

In the front part of the house, on the street-side and above the arrangement of bathroom on one side and dining room and kitchen on the other, there were two large beautiful rooms with four big windows onto the street. One of them was empty but quite soon would be occupied by a Czech girl, and later by Larry Powell—Lawrence Clark Powell—my friend from Occidental College. He came over a few months after we got there, to do his doctorate on Robinson Jeffers. Al's doctorate was on the comedies of Shakespeare.

The other room was occupied by the son of Monsieur Ollangier: Monsieur Jo, whom we soon came to know. He was an airy young man with delicate long hands and wavy hair which he kept shaking back. He was very soft and completely effeminate, rather wispy, and he plainly felt himself to be superior to most of the people of Dijon. He was a nice young man, but I never paid much attention to him because he never paid much attention to me. I think if I had not been there with my husband, I would have been more aware of him. But I was completely in love with Al.

Monsieur Jo decided to study watchmaking, so he was

5

apprenticed—because his father and stepmother said they could not afford University for him—to the leading clockmaker of Burgundy, there, in Dijon, who was the official keeper of all the town clocks and of the great Jacquemart, which was a mechanized clock high up on the façade of the église Notre-Dame. It was one of the famous ones in France. We went up into it later, with Monsieur Jo. It was a strange old clock with hammers and bells and four iron people: Two little children would walk out on the quarter hour and the half hour, and on the hour their parents would join them in a procession across the façade from one side to the other. The man was huge, twice life-size, and he would strike the hour, Bong! and the lady would curtsy and the children would bow. At noon, tourists would stop and gape up at the daily show, along with all the Dijonnais passing toward their homes for their noon dinners.

At the very top of the stairway on the third floor at the back of the house, in the attic of the house really, were the rooms that Madame Ollangnier had for rent. There were two tiny rooms, long and narrow, with the most hideous wallpaper I have ever seen. There was a big window in each room, looking down into the hard gray little court.

The entrance was at the top of the stairs, and in the back of them were a sort of storage attic and two miserable servants' rooms. The bedroom of the rooms for rent was papered in mustard and black stripes, about eight inches wide, with a wide band of American Beauty roses around the attic ceiling. It looked like marble—brown and mottled, orange and mustard—to tie the whole thing together, to make it elegant. And there was a pair of mustard-colored old tired velvet curtains across the window, with a little brown radiator underneath that made a terrible crashing and banging and hissing every morning, and since it sat right under the window the heat went right up and out the window.

There was a huge lumpy bed far at the back, and a big armoire at the foot of the bed, against one wall. The room could not have been more than nine feet wide and maybe eighteen feet long, with the window at one end and the bed at the other, with a little night stand on each side, of course. And there was a kind of recess, next to the armoire, where we were to hang our clothes. There was no chair or anything else in that room; there was no place for it.

The first little room led to the next smaller one, which was to become a "study" for Al because he was writing. The wallpaper in this smaller room was in several shades of purple and lavender, with brown accents . . . a more feminine *décor,* Madame Ollangnier pointed out. It was terrible, old and smudged and so French we loved it. There was a low armchair by another window radiator, and there was a makeshift bookshelf and an old wobbly table-desk and one straight kitchen chair. At the back of the room there was a kind of storage space where we would keep my steamer trunk and Al's steamer trunk and a couple of boxes of books and empty pieces of luggage. It seems funny, by now, that students owned such elaborate luggage. In those days, though, even if you went steerage, or "student third" as it was called, which we had done, you had steamer trunks; you had hatboxes; you had shoe boxes. And in Dijon that would all be put at the far back end of the purple "attic" sitting room. I think each room had one shaded lightbulb hanging down from the middle of the ceiling—awful, but I loved them. I loved everything about our quarters.

At the top of the stairs, outside the rooms and squeezed into a corner of the landing, there was a tiny little excuse for a *toilette.* It had a bucket with a cover, a little spindly dining room or kitchen chair, and a tiny counter with a sink and an oilcloth curtain hanging in front of it, under which the pee-bucket was supposed to go. There was a kind of sink with a rubber tube beneath the faucet, so that you could direct the cold running water into this dreadful little basin.

Beside this basin, to the right, there was a space for a one-burner stove and a box of matches, and that's where Al was to warm his shaving water in the morning, in a little saucepan. I bought another one soon for making tea.

MADAME PUSHED her hennaed hair back from her forehead, and I gave her all the money I had, even without getting my husband's opinion first, and said haltingly that we would arrive the next noon.

"We?" she said, with a sharp mocking voice that I was to know very well, and grow fond of.

"Yes . . . my husband . . . I am married."

She laughed loudly. "All right, all right, bring your friend along," she said, but there was nothing mean about her voice.

"*Voir, 'tite 'zelle,*" she called hurriedly and disappeared into the kitchen as I closed the door and climbed up into the waiting *fiacre.* But before we could start, she came shrieking out onto the narrow sidewalk, with a scrawled piece of wrapping paper in her hand, a receipt for what I had paid her.

I turned back to smile at her as we drove off. She was standing with one foot over the high doorsill, hands rolled in her apron, watching me with a mixture of affection and innate scorn, which I soon learned she felt for all creatures, but mostly humans.

CHAPTER

TWO

THE DINING room at the Ollangnier's was just large enough for a round table, six or eight chairs, and a shallow kind of cupboard with two small deer heads over it and an empty shell-case marked *Souvenir de Verdun* on top. It was an ugly little room, spotted and stuffy, with a cluster of mustard and spice pots on the dirty checked tablecloth.

There was the one picture on the wall, of Madame Bitsch, and it had glass on it that was spotted with steam and grease. The walls were dirty, just painted cement. The high barred window onto the street was always shuttered. It was dingy and terrible, but it was always very lively. There was a one-bulb light hanging down over the table, but that was all the light that was needed because the room was so small. Madame would do her accounts there at night and, when we would come in from lectures or movies, if the light was on, we would tiptoe past the door.

But the dining room was always pleasant while Madame was in it. Her wonderful honest vulgarity made us alive too, and after a meal, when she finally stopped pestering the cook and stretched her tired piano-teacher hands out across the cloth, her talk was good.

She was always late for meals; her pupils were for the most part young or stupid, and she was too much interested in even the dullest of them to send them off at the strike of the hour. Instead, she pounded out do-re-mis on the big piano under our rooms so long and so violently that from pure exhaustion the children grasped

11

their rhythmic monotony before she let them go home. Then she came running down to the dining room, the lines deep in her red face.

She was usually two courses behind us, but caught up with our comparatively ponderous eating almost before we could wipe our lips or drink a little wine, which on her instruction Monsieur Ollangnier tried to keep well watered in our tumblers. Madame Ollangnier ate like a madwoman, crumbs falling from her mouth, her cheeks bulging, her eyes glistening and darting about the plates and cups, and her hands tearing at chunks of cheese and crusts of bread. Occasionally she stopped long enough to put a tiny bite between the wet delicate lips of her little terrier Tango, who sat silently on her knees through every meal.

Under and around and over the food came her voice, high and deliberately coarse, to mock her prissy husband's Parisian affectations. She told jokes at which her own lusty laughter sounded in the hot air before ours did, or proved that Beethoven and Bach were really Frenchmen kidnapped at birth by the *sales boches.* She became excited about the last war, or the lying-in of a stepdaughter by one of her three other marriages, or the rising prices, and talked in a frantic stream of words that verged on hysteria and kept us tense and pleasurably horrified.

Her whole life was a joke, I think. She kept laughing and laughing, ribaldly, rowdily, coarsely, and also with great gusto and in a strange, refined way that was completely her own.

We were hypnotized, Al and I, and any other transient diners whose extra francs were so irresistible. Madame glanced at our faces as if we were her puppets, her idiotic but profitable puppets. Her eyes, amiably scornful, appraised us, felt the stuff of our clothes, weighed the gold in our rings, and all the time she saw to it that we ate better than any other *pensionnaires* in town, even if she did make more money out of us than any other landlady. I think we paid about twenty-five dollars apiece a month there, or a hundred francs, for room and board. It seems incredible now, but that was the way things were in those days.

We ate very good food indeed, but Madame Ollangnier was extremely penurious and stingy. Her reputation was a strange one, and everyone in Dijon knew her as the shrewdest bargainer, the toughest customer who ever set foot in the markets. One of her husbands had been a pawnbroker . . . but gossip said that she taught him everything he ever knew. She was supposed to be wealthy, of course, and I think she was.

She drove herself cruelly, and she was a tall and proud woman who looked younger than many women half her age, except for the hardness in her finely modeled mouth when it was still. She supervised the cooking, gave music lessons, played in the pit for visiting musical shows, and, if the leading man pleased her, slept with him . . . (gossip again) . . . and did all the marketing.

I was to learn, a couple of years later, that collecting enough food for even two people in a town the size of Dijon meant spending two or three days a week scuttling, heavily laden, from the big market, to the *charcuterie* around the block, to the *primeur*'s, to the milk shop. And Madame's system was even more complicated by her passion for economizing.

Storekeepers automatically lowered their prices when they saw her coming, but even so she would poke sneeringly at the best bananas, say, and then demand to be shown what was in reserve. Up would come the trapdoor to the cellar, and down Madame would climb, with the poor little fruit man after her. She would tap and sniff knowingly at the bunches hanging in the coolness, and then on her hands and knees, pull off the greenish midgets that grow along the stem at the bottom of the great clusters.

They were worthless: The man had to admit he gave them to his children to play house with. Into the black string bag they went, for a magnanimous twenty centimes or so . . . and in a few days we would have them fixed somehow with cream (at half-price because it was souring) and kirsch (bought cheaply because it was not properly stamped and Madame already knew too much about the wine merchant's private life). They would be delicious.

And while she was in the cellar she would pick up a handful of bruised oranges, a coconut with a crack in it, perhaps even some sprouting potatoes.

The little fruit man shook his head in an admiring daze, when she finally dashed out of the shop.

13

Even if Madame Ollangnier had been a Medici she would have been just as stingy. She loved it. She had a passion for making something out of nothing. People would say, "Oh, Madame Ollangnier's! You eat well there; tell us, what are you eating tonight?" People were fascinated by what we ate. It was so good to us, and very foreign—different from any food I'd ever had before. There were always great big salads which were made at the table, usually by Monsieur Ollangnier. He would put some olive oil and vinegar and mustard and a little salt and pepper in one big bowl, always a ceremony. Every noon we had a salad, either before the meat or after the meat, and cheese, always reject cheese and always very good.

We ate lots of Jerusalem artichokes, which were very cheap. They were delicious, and sweet, and they were usually deep fried, little crunchy things. We had them with cream now and then, and we had all kinds of little apples with wormholes in them.

Then there would be desserts, about which I don't remember very much. Monsieur would go to the *pâtisserie* on Sundays. All the men would be standing around with boxes from the *pâtisserie*. They would go to Mass, and then on the way home, stop at the bakery to buy the pastries. The baker would tie a little string around the box, and then the men would carry the boxes by the string, as if they were the sole providers for the Sunday luxury. In every French town I ever lived in, even when they couldn't afford it, the men would do this on Sundays.

Madame Ollangnier sometimes wore several diamond rings left to her by her late husbands, and when she was playing in the theater pit she had her hair freshly tinted and waved. The rest of the time, in the daily hysterical routine, her appearance meant nothing to her if it involved spending money. She had an old but respectable fur coat, but hurried around town in two or three or four heavy sweaters rather than wear it out, and when even they did not hold off the dank Dijon cold, she simply added more layers of underwear.

"Eugénie," her husband said one day, in his precise pettish voice, rolling his eyes waggishly, "it is hardly seemly that a woman of your age go around looking as if she were about to produce twins."

Jo flushed at the ugly reference to human reproduction. He was

14

accustomed to enduring in stiff silence his stepmother's vulgarities, but could usually trust his father to behave like a member of the upper classes to which they both so earnestly aspired.

Madame looked quickly at them. Two men, her eyes seemed to say, but neither one a man. . . .

She screamed with laughter. "Twins! No fear, Paul! The Dijonnais would never blame *you* for twins. If anything but a little gas should raise my belly, there would be more horns in this room than those on the deers' heads!"

Her eyes were screwed into little points, very bright and blue under the tangled hair. She was cruel, but we had to laugh too, and even Monsieur Ollangnier grinned and stroked his little moustache. He died every day ten deaths with her, but he always managed to keep things fairly genteel.

He accepted his advancing years grudgingly, and floated from one unmentioned birthday to the next on an expensive flood of "virility" tonics. Of course, the labels said "Rheumatism," "Grippe," "Gout," but we saw around him an aura of alarm: Eugénie stayed so *young.* . . . In spite of his Royalist leanings and his patent embarrassment at her robust vulgarity, he knew she had more life in her eyelashes than he had in his whole timid snobbish body. He took refuge in wincing at her Burgundian accent, and raising his dainty son to be a gentleman.

The kitchen was a dark cabinet perhaps nine feet square, its walls banked with copper pots and pans, with a pump for water outside the door. And from that little hole, which would make an American shudder with disgust, Madame Ollangnier turned out daily two of the finest meals I have yet eaten. But cooks found it impossible to work with Madame Ollangnier, impossible to work at all. She was quite unable to trust anyone else's intelligence, and very frank in commenting on the lack of it, always in her highest, most fish-wifish shriek. Her meals were a series of dashes to the kitchen to see if the latest slavey had basted the meat or put the coffee on to filter.

She could keep her eyes on the bottle that way, too. All her cooks drank, sooner or later, in soggy desperation. Madame took it philosophically; instead of hiding the supply of wine, she filled up the bottles with water as they grew empty, and told us about it loudly at the table, as one more proof of human imbecility.

"Poor fools," she said, her strong flushed face reflective and almost tender. "I myself . . . what would I be if I had spent my life in other people's swill? The only cook I ever had who didn't take to the bottle ate so much good food that her feet finally bent under when she walked. I'd rather have them stagger than stuff."

Madame herself drank only in Lent, for some deeply hidden reason. Then she grew uproarious and affectionate and finally tearful on hot spiced *Moulin à Vent,* in which she sopped fried pastries called *Friandises de Carême.* They immediately became very limp and noisy to eat, and she loved them: a way to make long soughings which irritated her husband and satisfied her bitter insistence that we are all beasts.

She let the little dog Tango chew soft bits from the dripping crullers in her big fine hands, and they both grew more loving, until finally poor Monsieur Ollangnier flounced from the room, *L'Action Française* or *Le Monde* tucked under his arm.

Madame loved boarders; they amused her, and brought in regular money, which became with her magnificent scrimpings a fat profit every month. When Al and I came we were the only ones, but in the next several months, before she had sold the whole house with us in it to the Rigoulots, there were probably twenty people who came and went, most of them foreigners.

Monsieur Ollangnier resented us all, but he was very nice to Al and me, especially me, because I was a good student at Beaux Arts. He was a really good architect and he knew a lot about it. Somewhere there is an old portfolio of mine simply because he said one hand I had drawn was good. (I did a lot with the figure but I always drew a tall, thin figure even when the subject was a little, squat person.)

Monsieur Ollangnier would always correct my French. He was very good about that and we never spoke a word of English. He would correct my accent in a kind way, and he introduced me to the name of Brillat-Savarin whose family came from Belley, his family home. Probably our dinner had been scraped up from the pavement somewhere, but refried and redone, beautifully cooked, and we all discussed it and Brillat-Savarin at great length. That was the first time I ever *talked* about food. At home when I was little we were allowed to say "Oh boy, this is *good!*" when Grandmother was not there.

He was courteous to us both and he and Al talked punctiliously about good writers and *L'Action Française,* as well as the Royalist politics espoused by that journal. He approved of our friendships with young members of the aristocracy, the *petite noblesse* of the town, and occasionally took us to his country places in his capacity as city architect, when there was room in the backseat of the car driven by his friend.

We spoke only when spoken to and absorbed a great deal of good French. I learned how to stand apart from the men when we stopped at the formal *châteaux* to taste wine in the cold courtyards outside the cellars. And I learned then that in some of the great cellars women were never allowed to enter because at certain times of the month the wine would turn in the bottles in their presence. I was always very careful never to set foot in the cellars unless I was specifically invited by the cellarmaster himself. It never seemed strange to me to stand alone, often ignored completely by the men, and I watched them from a distance and tried not to smile at seeing my husband trying to imitate their Burgundian mannerisms, as they got out the wine, until finally a good bottle was poured and they all smacked their lips and muttered as they tasted it and then swallowed.

The ceremonial visits to the country *châteaux* were rare but they were good training for us both, and we missed them when the Ollangniers moved at the end of our first year and left us as legacies to the Rigoulots.

"WAIT!" MADAME Ollangnier once shrieked at me, when she heard that in all my twenty-one years I had never heard a cuckoo. She looked challengingly at the polite faces of the other boarders. "The young lady is mistaken," she said flatly. "Here in France everybody has heard a cuckoo."

17

When I finally convinced her that in Southern California, which she always referred to as Northern Mexico, there were no cuckoos to hear, she said that the dreadful hiatus in my education must be filled up as soon as possible: The song of the cuckoo was without doubt the loveliest, most haunting, most melodious, of any bird's. It was *magical,* she said. And it was the first . . . it meant spring was here, and summer soon to come. Madame herself would take me to the woods, on the first warm day in April, and together we would listen until we heard that silvery fluting. . . .

The warm day finally came, and I skipped classes at school and Madame canceled two music lessons ("the little idiots wouldn't have practiced anyway," she said. "Spring fever . . ."), and we walked for several miles into the woods southwest of Dijon. We stepped softly over the moist earth, picking a few early violets and primroses, and listening with our innermost ears for the cuckoo's call. Madame had a look of almost exalted concentration on her hard sly amiable face. I was beginning to feel a little cold, and more than a little nerve-wracked by the whole business, when suddenly she threw back her head and let out a wild string of absolute gibberish. I leaped in my skin with fright. Visions of being hacked to bits by a madwoman in the lonely forest filled my head. Who would ever find me?

The violets shook in my hand, and I stared with horror as Madame yelled on. Just as suddenly as she'd begun, she stopped, laughed triumphantly, and said, *"There!* I'm rich for another year!"

"But . . ."

"The cuckoo, little stupid! Didn't you hear him? And of course, the more times you can say *money* before he stops singing, the richer you'll be!"

She put back her head again, to show me, and this time I could hear that she was shrieking "moneymoneymoneymoney," almost faster than her tongue could move. "It's a pity you didn't quite hear him," she added. "His song is without doubt the loveliest in the world."

My ears still rang with her wild shriek, and I began to laugh, remembering how William Wordsworth once asked:

O cuckoo! shall I call thee bird,
Or but a wandering voice?

"And now we'll have to trot," Madame said. "Suppertime soon, and since I feel so much richer, we'll open a bottle of sparkling wine tonight, my dear little North Mexican! Imagine, a country without a cuckoo!"

WE USED to sit there at the table after the noon dinner or on Sundays, and talk about the private lives of ghosts and archbishops and such. Occasionally, the cook would hiccup.

"You hear that?" Madame would interrupt herself. Then she would shout toward the kitchen, *"Imbécile!!"*

We would go on talking, cracking little wizened delicious nuts that had been picked up off the cellar floor of some helplessly hypnotized merchant. We would be pleasantly full of good food, well cooked, and seasoned with a kind of avaricious genius that could have made boiled shoe taste like milk-fed lamb *à la mode printanière.*

Maybe it *was* boiled shoe . . . but by the time Madame got through with it, it was nourishing and full of heavenly flavor, and so were all the other courses that she wrung daily, in a kind of maniacal game, from the third-rate shops of Dijon and her own ingenuity.

She would look at us, as we sat there cozily in the odorous little room, and while she told us the strange story of one of her pupils who ran off with a priest, her mind was figuring what each of us had paid her for the good meal, and how much profit she had made.

"Imbécile!" she would scream ferociously at another helpless hiccup from the kitchen. And when we finally left, she would dart to the sink, and we would hear her say, gently, "Girl, you're tired. Here's enough cash for a seat at the movie. Finish the dishes and then go there and rest your feet. And don't bring home any soldiers. Remember the so-called newlyweds are right next to you!"

Then Madame would laugh loudly and, if it was a Sunday, go to

her little *salon* and play parts of a great many things by Chopin . . .
all tenderness and involuted passion.

CHAPTER

THREE

I OFTEN sat in the window of the smaller of our two rooms, which we called the workroom or the purple chamber, and, very rarely during our first winter there, Madame Bitsch would come out into the courtyard, in a kind of long warm housecoat, on the arm either of her daughter, Madame Ollangnier, or of Marguerite (the first slavey I was to know there). She would call to the sparrows *"P'tit, p'tit, p'tit, p'tit,"* and they would come down and peck crumbs from her hands and arms. It was very touching and I wrote a little poem about it, which I never showed anybody.

The courtyard was perhaps fifty feet long and thirty feet wide, and it was surrounded by the house on three sides. The fourth side was a high wall, and I could see down and over it from my windows. There was nothing growing in our own courtyard. It was dull, not even painted, all barren cement and gray stone. And the wall was far too high for anyone to climb, but still it had the conventional broken glass along the top of it, in an ugly way that was peculiar to small-town French garden walls. On the other side, though, there was a formal garden with two little trees growing. It was part of the home of the Archbishop of Dijon.

I never heard a sound from over that high wall, and I saw the Archbishop only a few times. He was a tall man, gaunt and fair, and he was from Bordeaux. (Most of the Burgundians were short and dark, including the women.) The streets of Dijon were usually

slightly moist most of the year, if not icy, if not awash, and I remember that he seemed to wear something purple, maybe it was his
socks, and then large black shoes because he was a big man, tall, not
heavy. And on the bottom of the soles were two large crosses so that
every time he stepped he left their imprint. People would look down
stupidly watching his footprints on the pavement, and of course we
did not step where he had left his mark. This impressed me and for
some reason or other pleased me, but it also amused me and it still
does.

I used to watch the cars come down the rue Chabot-Charny to
the house across from ours . . . the house of Gaston Gérard. He was
a violently potent figure in the life of that region then, as the Mayor
of Dijon, and I used to peer openly at him from our rooms.

Many dignitaries and public figures visited there, so that often
there was a bustle on the street. Several elegant limousines would
draw up, and we would even hear music as the doors, the great
doors, opened and shut. Gaston Gérard would bustle grandly in and
out of his courtyard with people like Tardieu and prime ministers
and such.

He was a short, fairly thick man, and in 1954 when I came back
for the Foire Gastronomique, his fine dark moustache was frankly
tinted, his front hairs above his brow were most probably detach-
able, his teeth did not quite fit (because like most old men he hated
to spend money on a new set of dentures), and his trim middle was
probably bolstered by a band of boned elastic (the delight and reas-
surance of many a good man and woman besides this one). He still
was powerful politically and was famous throughout France for his
passionate insistence that the Foire Gastronomique would establish
forever the supremacy of Dijon as the gastronomical center of the
world. He had always been a flamboyant figure, and he never ceased
trying to prove that Dijon was more the capital of gastronomy than
Lyon. He started the Foire Gastronomique a year or two before we
first went to Dijon.

Occasionally, the doors of his house were left open, and I
would look inside as I walked to my classes at the University, and
I could see a pretty little courtyard, not built for carriages really. I
think there was a kind of room to the left of the door, probably for

the concierge, and then there was a wall with a very pretty fountain built out from it, and there were always pots of flowers blooming around it.

The house itself was gracious, rather like our own house but nicer, with high French windows on the ground floor. It was small, really basically a rather modest house, and the flowers were among the very few I ever saw in the nearly three years I lived in Dijon, except now and then around the fountains in the summer, for tourists I suppose. Dijon was really not a flowery city. It was ugly, as a matter of fact. The walls were always damp, and it was a gray, dim, dark town, very provincial. Of course, I loved it. I took it for granted, in a strange way.

From my window I watched every night for the streetlights to be lit. All the gas lamps on our street were lit by an old man, who came always from the direction of Chabot-Charny. They were lit at the same time every night, and in the summer they were on when they were not supposed to be and in the winter they would not go on until long after twilight.

One interesting thing that happened down in the courtyard was that a man came once a year and took all the stuffing out of all the mattresses, cleaned them, and then repacked them. He set up in the courtyard and did every mattress in the house. It took two or three days. We never spoke to him and he sat there day and night until he finished.

The view from my window down into the courtyard went directly to the door of the family latrine. It stood out from the Archbishop's wall and it was a pleasant little room, with one electric lightbulb in it and always the faint sound of the black rushing waters of the ancient Dijon sewer, which flowed beneath all the houses and was probably a tributary of the Saône River. There was a big pitcher of water, which Marguerite filled every morning. After the latrine was used water was poured in from the pitcher until it was clean. And I think there was a brush made of that stiff wiggly kind of weed used for household brushes in France; hard tiny wiggly strands. On the other side of the seat there was the French equivalent of the Sears Roebuck catalog that was supposed to be in every country privy in America, at one time. We tore out two or three pages, and it was probably good for my French, because of course I read it before I used it. It was not always the catalog; sometimes it was a newspaper torn into about four pieces, good too for a quick glance or two. Anyway, at the end of the daily performance a big handle at the back of the toilet was pulled, which flapped back the bottom of the toilet, and the contents went down into the flowing waters of the sewer.

There was also the bathroom on the ground floor, where Madame Ollangnier had assured me that for four francs, or three if we used our own soap, a bath could be drawn at only a few hours' notice.

I had one bath there, I think, but I laughed myself silly, so I went to the public baths like everyone else. Al would not reconcile himself to that and he was afraid to sleep with me for a month after my first visit, but everybody else went to them . . . working-class men, doctors, everyone, because there was simply no plumbing in the older part of Dijon. A tub had to be filled by hand and water had to be heated and carried to the room.

The public baths were ridiculously clean, and very properly run. There were little private rooms with a chair and a mirror and everything was painted white. A bath cost eight cents in 1929–1931. I always took my own soap and saved a franc, but the big towels were free. After twenty minutes an attendant would come and knock on the door and discreetly say, "Ten more minutes, Madame." Then there would be a rush to dry and dress before he came again to say firmly, "Out, out!"

I think the Dijonnais and the other French people I have known have been quite clean. Of course, after living in Dijon without the baths for quite a while, and in many other small French towns where the plumbing was definitely seventeenth century, I boast that I can bathe properly out of a teacup, for two or three years at a time.

CHAPTER

FOUR

THE FIRST night in the new quarters, after we had moved and arranged about having Al's trunks of books sent from the station, I looked up the word *anniversary* in my dictionary and told Madame that it was our first one. "Impossible," she shouted, glaring at me and then roaring with laughter when I said, "Three weeks, not even a month. We would like to go to a nice restaurant to celebrate," I said.

She ripped a piece of paper off a package on the wine-stained tablecloth, scrawled on it with a pencil stub she always seemed to have somewhere about her, and said, "Here . . . you know where the Ducal Palace is? The place d'Armes: You will see a sign there, the Three Pheasants. Give this to Monsieur Racouchot."

And she laughed again, as if I were amusing in an imbecilic way. I didn't mind.

We changed our clothes in the unfamiliar rooms. The lights were on wires with weighted pulleys, so that by sliding them up or down you could adjust their distance from the ceiling, and there was a kind of chain running through the socket of each one, which regulated the power of the light. There were fluted glass shades like pie pans, with squares of brown and purple sateen over them, weighted at each corner with a glass bead. The shadows in the unfamiliar corners, and on our faces, were dreadful in those mauve and mustard chambers.

But we felt beautiful. We put on our best clothes, and tiptoed down the wide stone stairs and past the lighted dining room, with a great key in Al's pocket and our hearts pounding . . . our first real meal alone together in a restaurant in France.

First we went up the rue Chabot-Charny to the Café de Paris, by the theater. It was Al's first love, and a faithful one. He worked there almost every day we lived in Dijon, and grew to know its waiters, the prostitutes who had their morning cards-and-coffee there, its regular patrons, and the rolling population of stock-actors and singers, who were playing at the theater across the street. It was warm in winter, and as cool and fresh as any provincial café could be in the summer. I liked it as soon as I walked shyly into it, that first night.

We were very ignorant about French *apéritifs,* so Al read from a sign above the cash desk when the waiter came, and said, "The Cocktail Montana, please." The waiter looked delighted, and dashed to the bar. After quite a while he brought a large tumbler, rimmed with white sugar, and filled with a golden-pink liquid. There were two straws stuck artfully on the frosted glass, one on Al's side and one on mine.

Al was a little embarrassed that he had not ordered clearly for both of us, but as it turned out, anything else would have been a disaster: The Cocktail Montana whipped up by the Café de Paris was one of the biggest, strongest, loudest drinks I ever drank.

We learned later that a traveling cowboy, stranded from a small Yankee circus, offered to teach its priceless secret to the café owner for free beer, promising him that Americans for miles around would flock to buy it . . . at nine francs a throw, instead of the one franc fifty ordinary drinks cost there. Of course, there were no Americans to flock; the few who stopped in Dijon sipped reverently of rare wines at the Three Pheasants or the Cloche, or good wines in any café, and would have shuddered with aesthetic and academic horror at such a concoction as we took turns drinking that night.

We enjoyed it immensely (we even had it once or twice again in the next three years, in a kind of sentimental loyalty), and walked on toward the Ducal Palace feeling happier than before.

We saw the big gold letters, Aux Trois Faisans, above a dim little café. It looked far from promising, but we went in, and showed Madame Ollangnier's scribbled note to the man behind the bar. He laughed, looked curiously at us, and took Al by the arm, as if we were deaf and dumb. He led us solicitously out into the great semi-circular *place,* and through an arch next to the café with two bay trees in tubs on either side. We were in a bare beautiful courtyard. A round light burned over a doorway.

The man laughed again, gave us each a silent little push toward the light, and disappeared. We never saw him again, but I remember how pleased he seemed to be, to leave his own café for a few minutes and direct such obviously bemazed innocents upstairs to Racouchot's. Probably it had never occurred to him, a good Burgundian, that anyone in the world did not know exactly how to come from any part of it straight to the famous door.

The first meal we had was a shy stupid one, but even if we had never gone back and never learned gradually how to order food and wine, it would still be among the important ones in my life.

We were really very timid that first time, but soon it all would become familiar to us. The noisy dark staircase and the big glass case with dead fish and lobsters and mushrooms and grapes piled on the ice no longer seemed strange to us. And after the first summer I never could pass the water closets with their swinging doors without remembering my mother's consternation when she had first entered them and found them full of men all chatting, easing themselves, and belching appreciatively. Her face puckered in an effort to look broad-minded.

The long hall past the kitchens and small private dining rooms and Racouchot's office, and the two dining rooms for the *pensionnaires,* then the dining room . . . I grew to know them as well as I know my own house now.

The glass door to Monsieur Racouchot's small and incredibly disordered office was usually closed, but we knew that it was often filled with the conglomerate cooking odors of a good meal being served to him and one or two of his cooks in their tall white bonnets.

The only regular *pensionnaires* we knew were Monsieur Venot, the town bookseller, from his shop on the corner two streets down on the place d'Armes, and one of the *Lycée* teachers, Jean Matrouchot.

As for the private dining rooms across the hall from the main

room, we seldom saw them except in passing. They were usually occupied by groups of wine men or famous politicians visiting the
Mayor, Gaston Gérard. Once or twice we engaged one to entertain
some of Al's friends from Princeton, who had come down from
Balliol College in Oxford, people like William Mode Spackman and
his wife Maryanne and her sister Dorothea, who had once been engaged to Al. We ordered especially good wines for them and I remember being much impressed when one of their guests grandly
reordered a bottle of the best wine we had yet dared offer to anyone,
a 1919 Gevrey-Chambertin of formidable reputation and equal
price. It seemed almost sacrilegious to me that anyone could be so
nonchalant about ordering so expensive a wine. I almost forgot their
pitying acceptance of our strange *toilette* in our apartment on the
rue du Petit-Potet, and I was glad to send them off filled with not
only Racouchot's fabulous wines but with his remarkable cuisine.

This long approach to the heart of the restaurant, the main dining room, was unlike any we had ever known. Always before we had
stepped almost from the street to a table, and taken it for granted
that somewhere, discreetly hidden and silenced, were kitchen and
offices and storage rooms. Here it was reversed, so that by the time
we came to the little square dining room, the *raison d'être* of all this
light and bustle and steam and planning, its quiet plainness was almost an anticlimax.

There were either nine or eleven tables in it, to hold four people, and one round one in the corner for six or eight. There were a
couple of large misty oil paintings, the kind that nobody needs to
look at, of autumn or perhaps spring landscapes. And there were
three large mirrors.

The one at the end of the room, facing the door, had a couple of
little signs on it, one recommending some kind of cocktail which we
never ordered and never saw anyone else drink either, and the other
giving the price by carafe and half-carafe of the red and white *vins
de maison*. As far as I know, we were the only people who ever ordered that: Racouchot was so famous for his Burgundian cellar that
everyone who came there knew just what fabulous wine to command, even if it meant saving for weeks beforehand. We did not yet
know enough.

We went into the room shyly, and by luck got the fourth table, in a corner at the far end, and the services of a small bright-eyed man with his thinning hair waxed into a rococo curlicue on his forehead.

His name was Charles, we found out later, and we knew him for a long time and learned a great deal from him. That first night he was more than kind to us, but it was obvious that there was little he could do except see that we were fed without feeling too ignorant. His tact was great, and touching. He put the big menus in our hands and pointed out two plans for us, one at twenty-two francs and the other, the *diner de luxe au prix fixe,* at twenty-five.

We took the latter, of course, although the other was fantastic enough . . . a series of blurred legendary words: *pâte truffé Charles le Témpéraire, poulet en cocotte aux Trois Faisons, civet à la mode bourguignonne* . . . and in eight or nine courses. . . .

We were lost, naturally, but not particularly worried. The room was so intimate and yet so reassuringly impersonal, and the people were so delightfully absorbed in themselves and their plates, and the waiter was so nice.

He came back. Now I knew him well enough to be sure that he liked us and did not want to embarrass us, so instead of presenting us with the incredible wine book, he said, "I think that Monsieur will enjoy trying, for tonight, a carafe of our own red. It is simple, but very interesting. And may I suggest a half-carafe of the white for an appetizer? Monsieur will agree with me that it is not bad at all with the first courses. . . ."

That was the only time Charles ever did that, but I have always blessed him for it. One of the great wines, which I have watched other people order there through snobbism or timidity when they knew as little as we did, would have been utterly wasted on us. Charles started us out right, and through the months watched us with his certain deft guidance learn to know what wine we wanted, and why.

That first night, as I think back on it, was amazing. The only reason we survived it was our youth . . . and perhaps the old saw that what you don't know won't hurt you. We drank, besides the astounding Cocktail Montana, almost two liters of wine, and then coffee, and then a little sweet liqueur whose name we had learned, something like Grand Marnier or Cointreau. And we ate the biggest, as well as the most exciting, meal that either of us had ever had.

As I remember, it was not difficult to keep on, to feel a steady avid curiosity. Everything that was brought to the table was so new, so wonderfully cooked, that what might have been with sated palates a gluttonous orgy was, for our ignorance, a constant refreshment. I know that never since have I eaten so much. Even the thought of a *prix-fixe* meal, in France or anywhere, makes me shudder now. But that night the kind ghosts of Lucullus and Brillat-Savarin as well as Rabelais and a hundred others stepped in to ease our adventurous bellies, and soothe our tongues. We were immune, safe in a charmed gastronomical circle.

We learned fast, and never again risked such surfeit . . . but that night it was all right.

I don't know now what we ate, but it was the sort of rich winy spiced cuisine that is typical of Burgundy, with many dark sauces and gamey meats and ending, I can guess, with a *soufflé* of kirsch and *glacé* fruits, or some such airy trifle.

We ate slowly and happily, watched over by little Charles, and the wine kept things from being gross and heavy inside us.

When we finally went home, to unlock the little door for the first time and go up the zigzag stairs to our own rooms, we wove a bit perhaps. But we felt as if we had seen the far shores of another world. We were drunk with the land breeze that blew from it, and the sure knowledge that it lay waiting for us.

We went back often to The Three Pheasants during the next three years, and in 1954, when I returned to the city for the Foire Gastronomique, I found that Racouchot had died and that his famous restaurant had been combined with the restaurant below it on the place d'Armes, the Pré aux Clercs. This was a good move, I am sure, but it never had the magic for me of the old restaurant upstairs. I remember dining there more than once with Norah when we went back during the seventies, and she agreed that it was by far the best place in Dijon, but it was never the same for me, and I remembered it as I had last known it.

CHAPTER

FIVE

N DIJON when Al and I were there, we were lucky to know people of almost every class, and to be within ourselves eager, interested, and above all husky-gutted. Most of our orgies were voluntary, but even so I doubt if more jaded livers than ours could have stood the thousand bilious blows we dealt them.

We went as often as we could afford it to all the restaurants in town, and along the Côte d'Or and even up into the Morvan, to the Lac de Settons, the Avallon . . . and down past Bresse. We ate terrines of *pâté* ten years old under their tight crusts of mildewed fat. We tied napkins under our chins and splashed in great odorous bowls of *écrevisses à la nage*. We addled our palates with snipes hung so long they fell from their hooks, to be roasted then on cushions of toast softened with the paste of their rotted innards and fine brandy. In village kitchens we ate hot leek soup with white wine and snippets of salt pork in it.

And in Dijon we went to Racouchot's, across from the Ducal Palace when we were flush.

In the railroad station at the beginning of the boulevard de Sévigné was the Buffet de la Gare, First Class. It had a good old reputation, and was nice in the winter because of the enormous iron stove as well as the ancient waiters and the bowls of flowers from Nice that conductors on the PLM expresses would throw off every day, probably in memory of good food they had eaten there. The Buf-

37

fet was especially proud of its *Tournedos Rossini,* which my husband liked very much, with its suave combination of fresh beef and almost putrescent *pâté de foie gras.*

Across from the station, at the beginning of the boulevard de Sévigné, was the Hôtel Terminus, with its large restaurant and the movie house behind it. It tried hard to bring a big-business Parisian atmosphere to Dijon, and failed completely. Its electric lights were all masked in slabs of cheap frosted glass cut on the diagonal . . . *l'art moderne,* the proprietor said proudly . . . and signs on the mirrors recommended regional specialties with a kind of condescending fervor. But the Dijonnais who had been reading *Le Temps* and *L'Intran'* under its lights since gas was first installed continued to go there . . . and the chef would always push aside his "Burgundian delicacies" long enough to make me a rum omelet, with three harsh scars of burnt sugar across its plump top where he laid the poker on to make an F for me. That was for a rare treat after the movies, which we went to often.

The main *café-brasserie* in Dijon in 1929 was called the Miroir, and it was very stylish and very big. It was down from the place D'Arcy on the rue de la Liberté near the corner of the rue Bossuet. That was one of the first cafés we went to, just because it was the biggest and the easiest place to find, and it was fun.

I remember the first thing Al ever ordered there was oysters, and even now oysters is hard to say in French: *huîtres-* . . . but he ordered a dozen. The waiter was not very nice; he teased and laughed, but Al did get a dozen oysters finally, and we ate them.

Good beer and good white wine were served there. *Vin Blanc Cassis* was a routine student's drink because it cost one franc. I think it was one franc twenty-five at the Miroir, which was the most expensive place. That was five cents then in our current exchange. We seldom had a real *apéritif* like a Dubonnet, because it cost one franc fifty to two francs. Now and then for a great treat I would have a Dubonnet and Al would have a Byrrh; they were stylish and they cost two francs . . . or one seventy-five . . . one seventy-five was seven cents.

The Miroir was one of the few cafés in Dijon big enough to hire a *chasseur,* one of those ageless little boys who used to scuttle around European *café-brasseries* with pen and paper, the dailies on long wooden sticks, cigars now and then, and messages for the bordellos. We knew Robert, although we seldom asked him for any services because we were poor.

He was about fifteen, with a wizened face and what was probably an increasing tendency toward epilepsy, if that can incease: We saw him go into a strange little dance twice or three times, when some fat customer had snarled at him. He would put up his two hands like a Balinese girl, and mince backwards a few steps, smiling and swaying, and then he would fall down. The waiters were kind to him, and would lift him swiftly to his feet again and hurry him toward the back of the big noisy room. He would always be smiling gently then, but when he saw Al and me, and was not near one of his little dances, he would grin like a gay ancient at us and put one of Al's cigarettes carefully into his round monkey cap.

During World War II the Miroir was taken over by German soldiers and it was very scandalous. When I went back after that, the Miroir was gone completely, because of its evil ugly reputation.

Down on the place d'Armes near Racouchot's, there was a restaurant, plain and self-contained in a deliberate way. It was called the Pré Aux Clercs, and Al liked to go there because it made very good grilled rare steaks with watercress, which at that time were beginning to be in great vogue in the big cities among the younger generation ... *"les sportifs"* ... but were dismissed with impatient disgust by older gourmands raised in the intricate traditions of fine sauces and culinary disguise. It was like the Chateaubriant at the other end of the town, also known mostly for its steaks and watercress and french fries.

Next to the Café de l'Opéra, facing the little place de l'Opéra, and down just about a half-block to the left of it, before the rue de la Liberté ended with the façade of the Church of Saint Michel, was the Café-Brasserie de Paris, where Al established himself. He thought it was part of the picture of being an American student in France, in those days, to establish oneself in a café. Of course, in Paris it was different; there were the Dôme and the Deux Magots, and many other fashionable student-tourist places. But there were no tourists at all in Dijon when we were there, as far as we knew anyway, and the students we knew were foreigners.

We were the only American students in the university, and there was only one other English-speaking person there at the time, an instructor at the Boys Lycée, a rather dull little Englishman. I think he was from the University of Manchester, and he was in Dijon doing his service. He spoke better French than he did English, but he had an ugly accent, I thought. We all spoke bad French together.

Al used to go every morning for almost three years to the Café de Paris, and he worked hard there writing sonnets and his great poem, *The Ghost in the Underblows*. (His friend Spackman later said it was gnomic. I did not know the word. . . .)

Al loved to talk with the prostitutes at the café, who went in there to have their coffee, during the morning. He loved prostitutes, as I was soon to learn. He loved to talk with them. I do not think he ever went with one to her chambers, partly because he was horrified by social diseases, but he asked all of them very intimate brotherly-fatherly probing questions.

Of course, the girls loved to talk with him and tell him what they chose to, about their lives and their lovers. And he fed on all this, and "knew" every whore in town.

I would come in after classes and we would have have an *apéro*. Of course, by then, all the whores had gone to work, and he felt safe to have his wife come along. Later Larry Powell, who was the only other American in Dijon . . . (After we'd been there I think about seven months) . . . would join us, and we became something of a fixture there, with our one morning drink.

One time Al read that Rimbaud and Baudelaire drank Pernod. So he wanted to try it. It cost a lot, we thought, but he ordered it anyway, at the Café de Paris, where they served it properly . . . with water and no ice. It was properly milky and probably very strong, although it was not the prewar kind made with wormwood that ate one's brain away.

But Al was convinced that his brain was being eaten away. One day Larry and I were walking home with him, and Al stopped and said, "I see tiny gnomes rising between the cobbles in the street." And Larry and I knew it was so phony that we broke out laughing.

We knew that Al wanted to see little gnomes, because he had been drinking Pernod for three days. Oh well, one Pernod, two Pernod, but never a rotted mind like those of some of the late nineteenth-century poets whom he hoped to resemble one day. So Al went back to *Vin Blanc d'Alsace* and his coffee.

There were places like the stand out in the park past the place Wilson, that made wonderful sandwiches of crisp rolls with loops and dollops of sweet home-cured ham in them . . . and the small restaurants along the Canal de Dijon that sold hot minnows, cooked whole and piled unblinking in a bowl . . . and little cafés that because their proprietors liked hot cheesecakes made hot cheesecakes once a week.

Then there was Crespin, the simplest and one of the best restaurants in the world. It was on one of the oldest streets off the place François Rude, between the markets behind the Ducal Palace and the church I liked the best, l'église Notre-Dame. In the winters an old oyster man stood outside always by his fish, stamping his feet like a horse and blowing on his huge bloody mottled hands. He was the best one I have ever seen for opening those devilish twisted shells, but still there was always a fresh cut somewhere on his grotesque stubs of fingers.

He had baskets of dark brown woven twigs, with the oysters lying impotently on seaweed within . . . Portugaises, Marennes, Vertes of different qualities, so fresh that their delicate flanges drew back at your breath upon them. Inside the little restaurant you could eat them with lemon and brown buttered bread, as in Paris, or with plain crusts of the white bread of Dijon. There was the classical green salad to scour the maw, and always a good plain tart of seasonal fruits if one could still face it. I remember some cheeses in the winter.

The small restaurant is gone now, but for a long time it served some of the simplest and lustiest meals I have ever eaten, especially on market days for the wine people who came in from all that part of Burgundy to talk about casks, corks, sulphates.

There were always snails at Crespin, in the cooler weather, and they were the best in the world, green and spitting in their little delicate coffins, each in its own hollow on the metal plates. After you pulled out the snail, and blew upon it cautiously and ate it, you tipped up the shell for every drop inside, and then with bread you polished the hollow it had lain in, not to miss any of the herby butter.

And then there were sealed casseroles of *tripes à la mode de Caen véritable.* Those casseroles, for two or six or eight people, seemed to possess the inexpressible cachet of a numbered duck at the Tour d'Argent, or a small perfect octahedral diamond from Kimberley. They were unsealed at the table. The vapor hissed out, and the whole dish seethed. Plates were too hot to touch bare-handed, to keep the sauce from turning as gluey as a good ox would need it to be (at a temperature more suited to his own digestion). It was served with soup spoons as well as knives and forks, and plenty of crusty bread lay alongside. It was a fine experience.

The last time I went there, I was alone. It was a strange feeling at first. I was in Dijon in 1954, to go again to the Foire Gastronomique. The town was jumping, quasi-hysterical, injected with a mysterious supercharge of medieval pomp and Madison-Avenue-via-Paris commercialism. I had gone to several banquets where ornate symbols were pinned and bestowed, with dignitaries several levels above me in the ferocious protocol of eating and drinking, and then I went by myself to the restaurant I wanted to be in once more.

I lied blandly and with a feeling of almost desperate urgency to my hosts, the Connes, hinting of final invitations to be accepted at the Fair, of obligations I must fulfill no matter how grudgingly, of appointments I must keep . . . all lies, lies. Georges and Henriette accepted them as such, with that impeccable and ironic grace which is all-French, all-Chinese, and I went off, feeling infantile, to keep an appointment I had made with myself. There was nothing really furtive about it, and I could easily have said the truth, that I wanted to dine *alone* in Dijon for once!

I headed unquestioningly for Crespin. I had noticed that neon now ringed the old sign saying "Oysters . . . Snails," but it had survived, like me.

The tall heavy old man with the scarred hands who used to open the oysters on the sidewalk was gone, but a sturdy boy did it just about as well, and inside there seemed to be no changes at all, except for new posters on the walls under the gas lamps saying that the *Chevaliers du Tastevin,* unborn when I first knew the place, considered it worthy of their patronage. I did too, and always had.

In the small, low room there was a great hum and fume, like market day but even better, and every table but one was occupied by large, red-faced, happy, loud Burgundians. My table was empty, and it seemed indicated by the gods that I had come to sit at it. I had sat there many times before, and never would again. It was a little apart but not obtrusively so, up a step, pleasantly enclosed on three sides, with the white window curtains at my back. If I had not come, a potted plant would have been set neatly in my place, I know. I felt pleased to be there instead, and as usual I was awed by my continuing good luck in life, especially now and then.

I settled myself comfortably at the table and picked up the menu with politeness, knowing exactly what I would order. This I did, and it was good: a dozen *Portugaises Vertes Extra,* then a dozen snails, then some ripe cheese from the Cistercian Abbey not far away. I drank a glass of dry white vermouth first, nothing with the almost violently alive sea-tasting oysters, and a half-bottle of red Meursault of a good year but somewhat disappointing. . . .

The heavy-legged kind waitress tended me with the slightly worried solicitude of a nurse whose patient looks normal enough but exhibits peculiar symptoms: Did I really want a red Meursault and not a white? And did I really want a *dozen* of *both* the oysters and the snails, no little grilled *biftec,* no *Coq au Chambertin?* And was I sure I meant the Cistercian or had I intended to say Camembert? Yes, yes, I said . . . red, yes, no, yes, and went on eating and drinking pleasurably, warmed by the being there even more than by the nourishment.

The wine picked up a bit with the cheese, and then *I sat back,* as I had done so often and so well in Crespin. Coffee was black and brutal.

Everything was as good as it had ever been some decades or centuries ago on my private calendar. Nobody paid any attention to my introspective and alcoved sensuality, and the general noise beat with provincial lustiness in the packed room, and an accordionist I had last seen in Marseille slid in from the frenzied streets and added to the wildness, somewhat hopelessly. When he saw me he nodded, recognizing me as a fellow wanderer. I asked him if he would have a drink, as he twiddled out near-logical tunes on the instrument he wore like a child on his belly. He looked full at me and said, "Some other time . . . a *pastis* at the Old Port."

When I went out toward the steep tiled roofs of the little square, and the narrow pushing roar of the rue de la Liberté, I could not know that the next time I returned, lemminglike, to the dank old town, Crespin and the white curtains and all of it would be gone, but it is. It is too bad to explain.

But everywhere in the first years when we were learning about noises, in every village pub or great temple of gastronomy, there were the proper wines, whether they came out of a spigot into a thick tumbler or slipped from a cradled cobwebbed bottle into the bottoms of glasses that rang thinly in the faintest stir of air. We grew to know, but always humbly, what wines of Burgundy and which years were regal, and how to suit the vintage to the hour. (Much of what I learned then I've forgotten. I feel it is a pity, but perhaps like any fish I shall remember how to swim if I am thrown back in the water before it is too late.)

Much of the time Al and I were learning and tasting all these things, we were living with the Ollangniers or the Rigoulots, so that some of our tutelage was of course involuntary. With them most of it, thank God, was good as well.

Of course I, as the wife of an almost-faculty-member, had to go to tea with my almost-colleagues much too often; I was young and felt earnestly that afternoons spent in the upstairs *salon* of Michelin's (on the corner of the rue Bossuet and the rue de la Liberté), eating almost unlimited pastries would help my husband's career. And once we had to go to a formal luncheon at the Rector's.

He was to French pedagogues what a combination of Nicholas Murray Butler and Robert Hutchins might be in this country, and Al and I were invited mainly because a visiting New England scholar had to be entertained. Like most ambassadors sent for one reason or another from America, he did not speak the language of the country he was to win to whatever cause he represented, and since I had gradually erased the firm impression among the faculty wives that all Yankee women either got tight in public on strange cocktails or spat in the drawing room, I was seated next to him.

He was a nice man, head of the English Department in a famous university. He had the same apparently instinctive naiveté of Wendell Willkie, which of course always wins people, especially when it is accompanied by slightly rumpled hair and a wide grin.

The luncheon was the most impressive private meal I have ever gone to. (Thank God, I add. I sometimes feel that I am almost miraculously fortunate, to have lived this long and never sat through one of the "state banquets" I have read about.) The Rector was noted for his table, but this time his chef had been helped by Racouchot, and several of the *restaurateur*'s best men were in the dining room with the butler and regular footman.

There were ranks of wine glasses, and the butler murmured the name and year of each wine as he poured it. Each one was beautiful.

All the ladies, including the hostess, wore hats, and some of them gloves rolled up around their wrists, and I felt slightly hysterical and almost like something out of Count Boni de Castellane's visits to Newport in the 1880s.

One of the courses was whole *écrevisses* in a rich sauce, served of course with the correct silver pliers, claw-crackers, gouges, and forceps.

The guest of honor was being very diplomatic, bending his white topknot first to the hostess and then to me, but when he saw the hard big coral fish lying in their Lucullan baths, he leaned against my shoulder and most unacademically he muttered, "Help, for God's sake, sister! What do I do now?"

I knew, because I had struggled before with the same somewhat overrated delicacy, and I had no practice with manmade tools in such emergencies. It would have been tactless for me to remind him that he could watch his hostess, so I winked at him and said, "Watch me."

I picked up a crayfish between my left thumb and forefinger, cracked both its claws with the silver crackers, ate what meat I could with the little fork, and then dunked the rest out of the sauce with a crust of bread. The visiting scholar sighed happily, and set to.

And that is the way everybody at the long oppressively polite table ate the rest of the course, and from then on things went fairly amicably and faculty feuds were forgotten or ignored, and at the end Madame la Recteur embraced me and made a date for tea.

(The whole incident sounds a little too charmingly barbaric . . . "these delightful American savages" . . . but I still do not believe that a host should serve anything that cannot be eaten with ease and finesse by all his guests who are reasonably able-bodied. In the case of *écrevisses* it is different of course when they are served with the claws cracked and the tails split. But in France it was felt, I think, that such sissy preparation ruined much of the flavor . . . and I have yet to see the most adept gourmet succeed in eating even one such crustacean with the prescribed tools. Cuffs rolled back, napkin under chin, an inevitable splash or two and more than that number of loud sucking noises: That is the routine at Prunier's, at the Rector's, and at the Café de l'Escargot d'Or down on the edge of any lake in crayfish season.)

Of course, there was the Foire Gastronomique every autumn, in Dijon: We went to the long tents and drank quite a lot of *vin mousseux,* but we were not important enough to be invited to any of the official banquets and could only read the fantastic menus in the paper. Prices went up for the visitors, most of whom were wine dealers, and gossip said that all the restaurants put an extra lot of seasonings in their sauces so that even mediocre wines would taste superlative. We liked Dijon better in its normal state of massgourmandise.

Probably the most orgiastic eating we did while we lived there was with the Club Alpin. Monsieur Ollangnier proposed us for membership soon after he had decided for himself, over the dinner table in his stuffy little dining room, that we were amusing and moderately civilized. It was supposed to be an honor, as well as making it possible for the club to get better rates on its feasts by having a large number of members, and certainly it was a fine although somewhat wearing experience for us.

We heard good French from the lawyers and retired army officers and fuddy-duddy architects like our friend Ollangnier who belonged, for one reason or another, but mostly gastronomic. We saw castles and convents and wine *caves* that were seldom bared to public eyes. We walked and crawled and slithered and puffed over all that corner of France, in the cold March rains, the winy gold-leafed days of autumn, April's first tantalizing softness.

We all had to wear properly stiff heavy boots, and on almost every one of the bimonthly promenades we managed to find a small safe grotto or gully to explore, so that the Alpin part of our club's name would not be too much of a joke, even in the heart of smooth-rolling Burgundy. The club's rooms in Dijon, on the ancient rue des Forges, were in one of the most perfect and beautiful fourteenth-century town houses in Europe, and we often listened solemnly to lectures there about the places we would visit in the future.

The real reason, though, for submitting to these often boring duties was that every time we spent half a day plugging doggedly across muddy fields and shivering in bat-filled slimy ruins, we spent an equal amount of time sitting warmly, winily, in the best local restaurant, eating specialties of the village or the region more ardently than ever peak was scaled or Gothic arch gazed on.

The schedule was always the same: a brisk walk from the station and the little train that had brought us from Dijon, four or five hours of eating and drinking, and then the long promenade, the climbing, the viewing of monuments and fallen temples. Al and I were probably the youngest in the club by some thirty years, but more than once pure bravado was all that kept us from tumbling right into the nearest ditch in a digestive coma. The colonels and counselors slapped their aged chests enthusiastically as the air struck them after the long hours in the restaurants, and they surged like a flock of young colts out into the country. We trotted mazily after them, two thin little American shadows convinced for a time at least that they were cousins of Gargantua.

The meals went on for hours, in spite of the length of the walk planned for later, and as a matter of pure research, based of course on our interest in folkways as well as culture, we arranged to taste not only the most noted dishes of the cook of the house, but also the Widow LeBlanc's way of pickling venison, and Monsieur le Curé's favorite recipe for little whole trout marinated in white wine and served chilled with green sour grapes.

The chef and his family would come in to enjoy our enjoyment,

and then Widow LeBlanc and the Curé and the Curé's cook, and all
of us would compare, with well-selected examples, the best local
and district wines for each course. We always paid due homage to
the ordinaries first, and then gradually lifted ourselves toward the
heights of local pride, the crowned bottles known to every connois-
seur alive, but never treated more respectfully than in their own
birthplaces.

Sometimes the mayor or the lord of the *château*, knowing the
Club Alpin of Dijon for what it really was, would send with his compliments a few bottles of such wines as I can only dream of now,
wines unlabeled, never tired by travels, inviolate from the prying
palates of commercial tasters. Then the gabble would die down,
and Monsieur le Curé would bend his head over his goblet as if he
were praying, and finally one or two of the old warhorses would
murmur reverently, with his eyes focused far inward, *"Epatant . . .
é-pa-tant!"*

The club secretary always tried to arrange our sorties so that
after we had studied a regional cuisine with the thoroughness it deserved, and had made solemn notes both physical and spiritual on
the vintages that flourished there, or there, or there, we could de-
vote ourselves with equally undivided zeal to the promenade itself.

More often than not, though, we would quite by accident find
that along with the *château* in a little village some two hours walk
past dinner, there was also a tiny pastry shop where a certain ancient
dame made sour-cream *fantaisies* the like of none other in all
France.

"My God," Monsieur Vaillant, the retired advocate, would cry,
halfway through our tour of a private country house where one of
Maintenon's exiled lovers had spent twenty leisurely years painting
Chinese pagodas on the wainscoting. "My God and double-zut!!
This is infamous! Here we are within ten minutes' delightful promenade from one of the great, the *great* pastry makers of all time! She is
modest, yes. She is content with a small fame. She made her
fantaisies for my dear mother's First Communion. They came in a
wooden trunk, packed in layers of silk-paper and dead leaves to survive the trip.

"Stop the tour!" Monsieur Vaillant would snort, his face

flushed with inspiration, and a dawning appetite in his rheumy old eyes. And he would send a boy ahead, to warn the old witch to start up her fire and bestir her bones.

And then after we had looked dutifully at the rest of the wall-paintings, and some of the more erudite had identified classical symbolism in the obscure little scenes, and some of the more lecherous had identified with equal pleasure a few neoclassical positions among the slant-eyed nymphs and mandarins, we would head for the pastry shop. Even Al and I would forget our surfeit, whipped by the clean air and Monsieur Vaillant's jubilant memoirs into a fresh hunger.

Sure enough, the toothless village heroine's sour-cream *fantaisies,* light, delicate, fried in pure butter to a color clearer than gold, paler than Josephine Baker but as vital, would be the most delicious pastry in all of France, and Monsieur Vaillant the proudest member of our club.

We'd drink hot wine . . . "Nothing better against these November winds," we agreed with Vaillant valiantly . . . and then climb up perhaps only three of the four hills planned on by the optimistic secretary, before we caught the stuffy train back to Dijon. We'd smoke and talk and doze, in that intimacy peculiar to a third-class French "local" on Sunday night, and never once did we regret in any way, digestive or moral, the day's licentious prodigality of tastes and sensuous pleasure.

Once a year, on Ascension Day, the club left all such energetic ideas of rising above the earth-level strictly to the church, and held its annual banquet without benefit of sortie, promenade, or appreciation of any well-preserved ruins other than the fellow members.

The only year I went to the Ascension Day banquet we dined for six hours at the Hôtel de la Poste in Beaune. That was long before the old place had its face lifted, and we ate in the dark odorous room where generations of coachmen and carriage drivers and chauffeurs had nourished themselves as well as their masters did "up front."

There was a long table for us, and an even longer one for the wines. Piles of the last year's grapes, kept carefully in straw, made the air tingle with a kind of decadent promise, but there were no flowers to interrupt our senses.

We toasted many things, and at first the guests and some of the old judges and officers busied themselves being important. But gradually, over the measured progress of the courses and the impressive changing beauty of the wines, snobberies and even politics dwindled in our hearts, and the wit and the laughing awareness that is France made all of us alive.

It seems strange, though, that of all the fastuous dining that we learned to take for granted on the Sundays with the Club Alpin, one of the meals I remember most clearly was early on in our membership. One bitter February Sunday when I stood panting on a hill near Les Laumes-Alésia, the earth was hard as granite beneath me, and air drawn into my tired lungs felt like heavy fire before it thawed. I broke a twig clumsily between my mittened fingers.

"Here!" a voice said, roughly. I looked with surprise at the old general, who stood, shaggy and immense, beside me. He had never done more than bow to me, and listen now and then with a face of stony suffering to my accent, which always grew ten times as thick when he was near. What did he want now?

"Here! Try some of this, young lady!" And he held out a piece of chocolate, pale brown with cold. I smiled and took it, resolving to say as little as possible.

He cleared his throat grumpily and shifted his eyes to the far thunderous horizon.

In my mouth the chocolate broke at first like gravel into many separate, disagreeable bits. I began to wonder if I could swallow them. Then they grew soft, and melted voluptuously into a warm stream down my throat.

The little doctor came bustling up, his proudly displayed alpenstock tucked under one short arm.

"Here! Wait, wait!" he cried. "Never eat chocolate without bread, young lady! Very bad for the interior, very bad. My General, you are remiss!"

The soldier peered down at him like a horse looking at a cheeky little dog, and then rumbled, "Give us some, then, old fellow. Trade two pieces (and big ones, mind) for some of our chocolate?"

And in two minutes my mouth was full of fresh bread, and melting chocolate, and as we sat gingerly, the three of us, on the frozen hill, looking down into the valley where Vercingetorix had fought so splendidly, we peered shyly and silently at each other and smiled and chewed at one of the most satisfying things I have ever eaten. I thought vaguely of the metamorphosis of wine and bread.

CHAPTER

SIX

WHEN I first went to Dijon in 1929, the rue de la Liberté was the main street in the old part of town. It split the town like a spine so that all life flowed on either side of it, and the life of the whole city was centered there.

Every settlement is divided into two parts by a main street, or even a river or a pathway. In Paris, for instance, the Seine River divides Paris into a left bank and a right bank, just as the main street in any small American town separates it into the right part and the left part of town . . . culturally, socially, economically, physically, statistically, and in every other way.

In Dijon, which was a small city but one of the oldest and noblest in a very old country when I went there in 1929, the rue de la Liberté divided the town inevitably, although it may not now be the center it once was.

Its narrowness did not adapt itself well to the increasing traffic, since it had existed since the Romans first built a fortified wall around a small camp. In medieval times it was crowded and not as crooked as many, and it was a thoroughfare long before automobiles, tramways, and buses tried to crowd its constant stream of travelers onto the narrow sidewalks. In 1929, though, it was still the main street of the town, and it cut like a sword through the thick conglomeration of small streets spreading out on either side of it.

After the railroads came to France and the PLM was finally completed connecting Paris and Marseille to the south, with Dijon the first main stop, the station was built at the edge of the walled town, and the street that led from it was called the boulevard de Sévigné. This wider street, lined with beautiful trees, was by far the most modern part of town, and it ended at the *Grand Place d'Arcy,* which continues now to be the center of the town, with the Bureau of Tourism located in its public gardens.

Somewhere on the place d'Arcy was an Arc de Triomphe, and it seems odd that I do not remember anything about it now, but the small Arc is an important part of the decor, especially because it was reported to be the model of the Grand Arc de Triomphe in Paris. It was designed by François Rude, one of the great sculptors; and it forms a part of the solid reputation of architecture and sculpture which has always made Dijon the center of Burgundian culture.

In 1929 the place d'Arcy served as a liaison between the old and the new parts of town, and contained the leading movie theater as well as the Hôtel de la Cloche and several bright *café-brasseries.* It was the entrance to the true old town and the rue de la Liberté.

The largest movie theater in town was the D'Arcy on the place d'Arcy. It was the kind where they rang the bell fifteen minutes before the movie, to notify people that it was time to come along, and then rang the bell again for the *entracte,* and it seemed to be heard all over town. The people would wander out to the cafés nearby and then they would come back to see the second half of the show.

Al loved the movies. He hated to stay home, and he believed very sincerely that we went to improve our French; because, first, there were subtitles, and then later while we were there, there came the sound pictures, in about 1931. We saw all the early Pagnol, and the Jean Giono stories that Pagnol made. We saw everything that was going . . . German films, the UFA films . . . we knew all the French and all the Italian films, which had subtitles in French. It was fun, but I got really fed up with going every single night to the movies. But Al loved it.

There was another theater in the back of the Grande Taverne restaurant, with the Hôtel Terminus above the two, on the top two stories of the same building. This theater was more like a music hall, however, with tables and one act of vaudeville. It was the first place that had a movie with a soundtrack. I had already seen the Al Jolson movie called *The Jazz Singer* when I came back to this country in 1931 and recommended it to several people who found it very puzzling: The soundtrack was to *The Jazz Singer,* with Al Jolson singing "Mammy," and the movie was called *The King of Jazz,* with Paul Whiteman and his full orchestra.

There was another smaller movie house way up on the place Grangier, and it showed rather offbeat movies, like all of Charlie Chaplin's, which I saw for the first time in years. We saw horror pictures there, and westerns.

On one side of the place d'Arcy, on the rue Victor Hugo facing the municipal gardens and the fountain, was the Hôtel de la Cloche, the Ritz of the town, and opposite it were the newspaper offices and two or three older hotels.

We stayed at the Cloche for a few days before moving to Madame Ollangnier's on the rue du Petit-Potet, mainly because it was the biggest and best-known place in town. We had known little then to appreciate its famous cellars, and had found the meals fairly dull in the big grim dining room. Later we learned that once a year, in November for the Foire Gastronomique, it recaptured for those days all its old glitter. Then it was full of gourmets from every corner of France, and famous chefs twirled saucepans in its kitchens, and wine buyers drank Chambertins and Cortons and Romanée-Contis by the *cave*-ful.

But for us it was not the place to be in 1929. My mother and sister Anne later stayed there for a few days when Mother came down from London with a bad knee the first summer we were there. She soon grew bored with it and moved to the Central, which was comparatively new and not really stylish in those days. And later Timmy, my second husband, and I stayed there at the Cloche with his mother, who loved its provincial elegance.

The boulevard de Sévigné and the rue Victor Hugo came to a point in front of the Hôtel de la Cloche where the gardens were, and then the place d'Arcy opened at its other end into the rue de la Liberté. The rue de la Liberté went past the Ducal Palace with its parade grounds in front, and ended naturally at the Church of Saint Michel.

It seemed very narrow always, especially the first long block that split off from the place d'Arcy, and it was in direct contrast to the wide boulevard de Sévigné which led directly from the station to it.

We smelled Dijon mustard, especially at one of the most important corners of the rue de la Liberté, where Grey-Poupon flaunted little pots of it. And I remember that long after I was there, my nephew Sean and his wife Anne and their two little boys were in France one year, and I had told Sean about the Grey-Poupon shop . . . a kind of showplace, with beautiful old faience jars in the windows and then copies of them that one could buy for mustard pots.

The two boys were fascinated, because they said the floor opened, and their clerk simply disappeared down into the basement right in the middle of the store. Of course, I was not surprised, but the boys were, and they waited, and finally the little man popped up again with a small *moutardièr*. I broke the bottom of it about three years ago, but I used it until then for mustard, and I still have its top, I believe, and the little wooden spoon with the blue ball on the end of it. It was darling, and they brought it clear from Dijon to me. I liked that. . . .

We smelled Dijon cassis in the autumn, and stained our mouths with its metallic purple. But all year and everywhere we smelled the Dijon gingerbread, that *pain d'épice* which came perhaps from Asia with a tired Crusader.

Its flat strange odor, honey, cow dung, clove, something unnameable but unmistakable, blew over all the town. Into the theater sometimes would swim a little cloud of it, or quickly through a café gray with smoke. In churches it went for one triumphant minute far above the incenses.

At art school, where tiny Ovide Yencesse tried to convince the hungriest students that medal-making was a great career, and fed them secretly whether they agreed or not, altar smoke crept through from the cathedral on one side, and from the other the smell of *pain d'épice* baking in a little factory. It was a smell as thick as a flannel curtain.

We knew most of the shops, and although I can't remember eating much gingerbread when we first went there, later when my younger sister Norah lived nearby, I bought it often. It was called *pavé de santé,* and it was the plainest and the most delicious, and the cheapest cut. It was made in huge loaves about six feet square, six inches thick, and it was sold in square blocks of about a kilo each, or a half-kilo maybe, and wrapped up in paper marked Mulot et Petit Jean or any of the other good gingerbread places. The smells were heavenly.

Mulot et Petit Jean was the biggest and oldest supplier of gingerbread, and its main store always looked something like a pharmacy. The women who worked there all looked the same, with tight high-breasted bodies and handsome hands and feet, and they went lightly over the tiled floors, behind the high polished counters piled with pretty boxes and the towering cash desk with a little carved fence around its top. They were deft and remote, and yet protective. Now and then for Christmas or birthdays, I sent loaves of the plain kind of gingerbread and boxes of the sticky kind to America, and they advised against shipping a round cake covered with candied cherries, and advised for a smaller square one stuffed with apricot jam, and I smiled at them without their knowing why, nor caring.

The Grey-Poupon shop was on the corner of one of the streets that led off the rue de la Liberté down to the place Bossuet, where Mulot et Petit Jean was, and across from it was a wonderful store where workmen got their clothes. Al bought a suit there, I remember. It was a navy blue corduroy, a thick-waled corduroy. One time there was a masked students' ball given by the Mayor in the Ducal Palace, and we both bought harlequin costumes alike there. I skinned my hair back, and was perhaps a little masculine. Al was rather effeminate, I think. Anyway, we both wore makeup, and he, to me, was obviously a man and I was obviously a girl, and it was fun.

The shop also had smocks for various kinds of working people (they all had their own smocks, navy blue, or dark gray), and there were lots of butchers' aprons. Every kind of workman had his own quality and cut and color of suit. I still have a smock that I bought there. It is gray and ugly, but I still have it hanging in my closet. I haven't worn it for years, but I keep it, for some reason. It would be a nice thing for a sculptor or cabinet worker . . . something to wipe gluey old hands on . . .

There were people who belted out street songs in 1929–1930. There were usually two people: One would be a wounded veteran from the war—World War I, which was still very keen in their minds, of course—and then there would be a woman. The man would sit on a little stool usually, and the woman would go around and collect pennies and sell sheet music now and then. They would sing a song, and sometimes they'd sing two or three, but they would sell the sheet music to people for a penny. I always stopped and listened, but it seems odd that I don't remember ever paying for and getting a piece of sheet music.

The Ducal Palace was at the far end of the rue de la Liberté facing the place d'Armes, and it was a series of majestic buildings, which housed the mayor's offices as well as the museums. In its courtyard was the Ducal Kitchen, which was nothing but a great chimney rising from a space which formed the oven itself.

There were several other things in the courtyard, including the brooding statue of Claus Sluter, the first great sculptor of Burgundy, who did the Puits de Moïse, which is outside the town. The great tower of Phillipe Le Bon was toward the back of the high buildings and rose high above even the churches. The rue de la Liberté separated the Ducal Palace from the place d'Armes, which was its natural parade ground and always seemed the center of town.

Down the rue de la Liberté from the Ducal Palace, there was the Opera House, the place de l'Opéra, and the small Café de l'Opéra. There was also a famous printshop, where they printed James Joyce, D. H. Lawrence, and other writers forbidden in America and England. There were strange typos in them, because all the proofreaders were, of course, Frenchmen speaking English. They finally did print Al's thesis and later Larry Powell's, because printing theses was their livelihood. Then there was the grain market, and on Wednesdays and Saturdays there would be lots of pigeons walking around, picking up seeds that the merchants had dropped from their pockets.

Behind the Ducal Palace ran the oldest marketing street in town. It was very narrow and crowded and dirty, and it was the most picturesque part of town, with gabled buildings showing the famous tiled roofs of Burgundy . . . green and yellow and black and red. And there was the beautiful small place François Rude and finally the place where people gathered to see the famous gargoyles and the great clock Jacquemart with its mechanized figures on the façade of the église Notre-Dame.

The other half of the ancient city was where the place d'Armes spread out in front of the Ducal Palace. Out from the half-circle of the *place* ran a dozen small streets which led into the older quarter of the city, part commercial and part beautiful town houses, which seemed to end for us anyway on the corner of the Chabot-Charny and the rue du Petit-Potet.

The buildings on the place d'Armes were all two-stories tall and fairly uniform, and they included several small cafés and tea shops and two restaurants, the Prés aux Clercs and Racouchot's Three Pheasants. On the corner of one of the streets that went down from the *place* was Venot's, the main bookstore of the town. It was the only one known to me then, and it supplied all the university books.

Monsieur Venot was a town character and was supposed to be the stingiest and most disagreeable man in Dijon, if not in the whole of France. But I did not know this, and I assumed that it was all right to treat him as if he were a polite and even generous person. I never bought much from him but textbooks, because I had no extra money, but I often spent hours in his cluttered big shop, looking at books and asking him things, and sniffing the fine papers there, and even sitting copying things from books he would suggest I use at his worktable, with his compliments and his ink and often his paper. In other words, he was polite and generous to me, and I liked him.

When I told that to Georges and Henriette Connes, many years after I had stopped being a student, and after old Monsieur Venot had died and left a lot of money to a host of people nobody ever knew he would spit upon, they laughed with a tolerant if amused astonishment; and of course I too know that by now I am much shyer than I was then, or perhaps only less ignorant, and that I would not dream of accepting so blandly an old miser's generosity and wisdom.

In Monsieur Venot's shop I learned to like French books better than any others. They bent to the hand and had to be cut, page by page. I liked that; having to work to earn the reward, cutting impa-

tiently through the cheap paper of a "train novel," the kind bought
in railroad stations to be thrown away and then as often kept for
many years, precious for one reason or another. I always liked the
way the paper crumbled a little onto my lap or my blanket or my
plate, along the edges of each page.

All the streets of this old quarter off the place d'Armes were
narrow and crooked and teeming with life behind their shuttered
windows, and from our rooms on the rue du Petit-Potet we could
hear fourteen or more bells ringing from the many small churches
and convents. Between our house and the place d'Armes there was
the Palais du justice, which always filled me with a feeling of horror
for the crimes that had been tried there for so many centuries. It was
a very old and noble building, though, with a great hall made all of
wood. Some of the streets in this part of the city had names like the
Street of the Good Little Children; and they became more familiar
to me than any I would ever know. Later when we moved to rue
Monge we were still in the older part of the town but down by the ca-
nals and the River Saône.

The town was to become more familiar to me than any other
place I had ever lived in before, or since. And I feel I could survive
there now as easily as I did the first three years, in spite of the inevitable changes that the short time of some sixty years can make in a
place even as old as Dijon was and is.

CHAPTER

SEVEN

BEAUX ARTS, the school, was perhaps two or three squares away from where we lived on the rue du Petit-Potet, across from the place Bossuet and down the rue Cardinale. It was part of the national system, and I think I paid a franc a night tuition.

The school was a beautiful austere building next to the ruins of an old church, built to house visiting church nobility in a proper style. There was a cobbled courtyard, and inside, the doors and halls and windows were tall and wide, as befitted ecclesiastical as well as fashionable rank, and the backside looked down on the remnants of a once elegant park, where indigent students from the university lived in run-down town houses.

At first, I went only to night classes at Beaux Arts. There was never any thought of street trouble in those days, some ten years after World War I, and I set off with my portfolio of drawing paper, and a pocket full of sharp pencils, under the lamplight. It never occurred to me that anyone would ever molest or bother me in any way. The streets were as safe at night as they were in the day. I suppose you got what you looked for, and I did not look for any trouble.

Tango, the Ollangnier Boston Terrier-of-sorts always came along, and when the classes were over and the lights went off in the big building after the last students had gone out the gates, Tango would be there waiting to walk home with me. He loved our route, along small streets where lights shone up through the sidewalk from underground bakeries. The bakers were all working under the sidewalks, under the shops. Sometimes, in the hot nights, the iron doors that were set in the sidewalks, would be open for air. I would look down, and the head of the young baker would pop up, usually with two pink cheeks, flour in his hair, flour in his eyelashes, having a cigarette outside the bakery, with the baking going on down below. Bright lights, lots of flour in the air, flour on the floor. The ovens were roaring and the flour was flying.

Tango left his calling card on as many lampposts as any dog who ever trotted along the damp but odorous streets of town, and once for fun I counted his successful visits to twenty-seven between Beaux Arts and the rue du Petit-Potet . . . a drop here, a drop there, doggedly.

After one semester of night school, I went to the morning classes five days a week, and I made a few good friends there. The night classes at school were warmer than the morning ones, because of all the people who had been breathing there in the great rooms.

The head of the Ecole des Beaux Arts was a pointy-bearded man who was an expert watercolorist and courtier of local patronesses. He came in once or twice during the morning classes, and breathed expensive mouthwashes down our necks as we sat before our easels. Now and then he gave a show in town, of pretty paintings. I think he had won a Prix de Rome much earlier. He was the boss of the Beaux Arts sinecure, but nobody paid much attention to him, which explains some of his invisibility.

Ovide Yencesse was the other half of the Beaux Arts *faculté*. He taught sculpture, and that was important: In 1929 there were many unregistered Italians and their children in Burgundy, and they seemed to feel that the best way to stay functioning without a passport was to carve tombstones. So Yencesse's classes were almost solely of beautiful young men who had to carve angel-faces and floating lilies, whether or not they could cut their own salami and cheese.

I worked for several months in the upstairs studios of the pointy-bearded director. A little wood stove was somewhere in the main corridor of the former palace of the cardinal, and the model was supposed to undress there and then walk through two huge "audience chambers" without even a towel, before he stepped up onto a platform before what, when I was there, was a gaggle of socially acceptable young ladies of Dijon, ranging from twenty-six to perhaps forty years old.

I was very shy, but I was accepted, and Al and I were drawn into a set of the young aristocracy of Burgundy: *la petite noblesse*. Today these women would be going to cooking schools. Then the only cultural outlet was Beaux Arts . . . unless, of course, a girl felt closer to The Church, whether single or married, and went in for Good Works.

Monsieur Ollangnier guided me deftly into night classes and then full mornings at Beaux Arts. Occasionally I would show him my dreadful drawings, and almost always he would find one small spot, like a pea in a bowl of porridge, that he could commend me for. As an artist I was plainly nil, but socially it made him feel good that the pointy-bearded man had found me potentially admissible to his morning classes.

I learned quite a lot of grammar there, all upper-bourgeois, as I solemnly drew feet, hands, arms, finally the frigid model's whole body.

I noticed that his skin was usually of a peculiar texture that only goose pimples can induce. The man was freezing, but gallant. He was usually a well-built Italian worker without a job, fairly clean, quite obviously shy and awkward. A few times he, whoever he was, would look around at all those half-frozen Burgundian females, and go into a strong erection, and have to stride out into the corridors of the Cardinal's Palace and come back sooner or later, pale and sheepish.

As I report this, I wonder at the reactions of the other students. My own were nil . . . a mild but not empathetic pity.

On Monsieur Ollangnier's suggestion, after about four months of this cultural induction, I shifted from anatomy to sculpture, under Monsieur Yencesse. His boss had never really recognized models, so why not work more with my hands and learn how to construct a wire armature?

Ovide Yencesse was one of the smallest men I ever met, made delicately of fine and perfectly proportioned bones. He moved the same way he was made, with precision and balance. He was a young Charles Chaplin, even in his sixties. As I see him from so far away, he was gray, neatly bearded, fastidiously dressed. He welcomed me casually to the big studio down the great icy halls from the watercolor and "life" classes run by his boss, and I felt I was in a better kingdom.

Sometime in our fleeting lengthy intense acquaintanceship, he said that the reason he was one of the best medalists in France, asked to design gold buttons to pin on national heroes and to commemorate great battles and events, was that he was too small to wield a chisel properly. And what is a sculptor of enormous monuments without his chisel and his mallet and the strong long arms to wield them, and the long legs to climb spidery scaffoldings?

He could design monuments, but he could not execute them. He was a ridiculous gnat on those great blocks of marble that France and other countries were erecting to celebrate themselves. . . . His salvation, he said, was to think of his wife whenever he found himself astride a great granite nose or hand. So he chose to carve tiny exquisite medals, which in the right perspective became as massive and subtle as any village or city triumphal arch.

He was married to a woman I never met, although I could have, who bore him a big brood of fine healthy tall large children. I forget how many there were . . . ten or twelve.

They lived in a somewhat legendary villa outside of Dijon. Once I was invited there, but I did not understand the smiling words about coming in on Sunday between three o'clock and six o'clock, and when Monsieur Yencesse asked me politely why I had not appeared, I was so confused and embarrassed that I pretended to be totally unwitting about the whole thing. He shrugged a little, and I was not asked again to what I later learned were very rare bids to Sunday afternoons filled with dancing, good wine, and dozens of young people learning how to get through the next week, the next exam, the next *day*. I was learning all this too, and have always been sorry that I could not have perhaps got a few pointers from the reportedly uninhibited young people *chez* Yencesse.

Pierre, one of the sons, was helping his father at Beaux Arts. I do not know what "helping" means, but he had a studio upstairs in the old cardinals' rooms, and one time at an exhibition of young artists' work in Dijon, he showed a sketch of a fat ugly and surely smelly girl sprawled out that was so compellingly good that, for the first time in my life, I knew that I should mortgage my future to own a picture.

It had already been sold when I asked to speak to Monsieur Pierre. He looked at me with amusement, and said he was astonished that I would be interested in a female body like the one in his drawing. Could he send me a photographic copy of it? I stumbled out, feeling clumsy and stupid. He thought I wanted it for reasons that I did not know, for its subject and not its *maîtrise*. I could never explain it to anyone. He sent me the copy, which I still have and which is one of those masterly things that happen at least once in an artist's life. Perhaps Pierre did not want to admit that I had caught his flash? My recognition of that was intuitive, and I am glad it surprised him, no matter what he may have surmised about my wanting it. (It is hard and perhaps impossible for many people to recognize the difference between innocence and naiveté.)

So I continued for the second year at Beaux Arts in Ovide Yencesse's sculpture class, every morning for five days a week. It was fun. I stayed silent and aloof, but was very aware of the enormous rooms, the wonderful light. It was with young men learning how to carve tombstones, and they were polite and handsome, but we did not exchange more than two real words in a morning. (I was an American, and I was married: enough!) Finally I realized that they resented me. I was a female but I was completely apart, not interested, not bothered by their maleness. This was puzzling to them.

Once I went into the *atelier,* after changing as usual into my long smock, or whatever that heavy uniform is that was worn then in sculpture classes, and every clay model in the room, where we had all been working on a male human form (no models, this time!) had a big firm handsome banana for a penis, instead of the discreet little dangling clay forms or leaves that had been there.

One of the silent impersonal students went around the studio and removed the fruit. I doubt there were any snickers, but soon Monsieur Yencesse asked me to come with him out into the long gallery where several tubs were kept busy watering the clay we used.

He showed me that my armature and table and so on had already been moved out there, next to a clay-tub. He said he thought it might be easier for me to work without the pressure of the professional speed of the tombstone boys.

I never made anything worth talking about: a couple of bas-reliefs, since I respected Ovide Yencesse's exquisite mastery of this strangely subtle and limited skill, and then one small head, in the round, of my sister Norah. I never communicated with the man, by mail that is, and can only remember something sad in his tiny shrug when he asked me why I had not come out to the Sunday frolic. I would have loved to. But I honestly did not understand that it was a royal command from someone I look back to as a powerful figure, able to carve great monuments except for his tiny hands, his short frail bones. He, and his son Pierre, and perhaps the unsmiling students at the last, gave me a better education than I deserved.

CHAPTER

EIGHT

AL WAS basically a teacher-type and he would bring me home a book and say, "Now you translate that." And I would.

He brought me one book about El Greco; another about Dürer. Soon I began to exchange French for English, recommended by the man who had found our lodging, Monsieur Martenot, at the student placement bureau. He got two or three very nice young ladies to come to my apartment, which was permitted because I was married. If I had not been married, we would have had to meet either in one of the classrooms at the school or at the students' gathering hall which was behind Beaux Arts, a beautiful place but filled with very poor foreign students, who lived there for fifteen cents a day for food—terrible food—and lodging. Of course I had the little gas grill in the toilet, and so we would make tea, and I would run out for some cookies or cakes. Or, now and then the girls would bring me some, or we would go out to tea at Duthu or Michelin when we were in funds.

It seems strange that I do not remember much about the classes at the university. I followed them for three years and they were too easy for me, as they have always been, so that when I took the public examinations at the end of my second year, I was really taken aback to find my name in the paper along with all the other students, but halfway down the list instead of at the top. That meant that I was not a good student at all.

The *assez bien* that followed my name still hurts me. It was the only time in my life when I have been publicly called "good enough," and not *très bien*. It was a real shock to me, and for the first time I looked at my own performance with new humility. I had simply breezed through courses with my usual nonchalance and that *assez bien* was my comeuppance. I realized then that I had never studied in my life, and never again would. I had had a chance to prove that I could work hard and perhaps earn the A's that I had always taken for granted. My teachers were patient with me but did not take me seriously, and why should they. I was plainly a dilettante to the fine men who tried to teach me.

One of the most important professors at the *faculté* was, of course, Georges Connes, since he was in charge of the doctorate Al was studying for (and later was the mentor for Larry Powell); and we were often guests in his house during the three years that we lived there. We were perforce invited to several stuffy dinners there in the villa during Al's studies under Connes. They were by far the most painful ones I had gone to since my own days as a boarding-school girl, and I felt all my old shyness and awkwardness. But I enjoyed them for Al's sake. It is good to note now that much later I could return to that house as a mature friend of both Georges and Henriette.

Georges was a tall, spare man with oversimple manners, as if he were compensating for the superior manners of his wife, Henriette Le Gouis Connes. She was for years a person of some terror to me, which I blamed partly on her manner of severity toward Georges.

She was head of the English Department at the Lycée des Jeune Filles for as long as I knew her. That, fortunately, was for many years after we left Dijon and my first terror of her changed into a real friendship, and her cold superior manners became more friendly. Fortunately, she had nothing to do with us, as we were in Georges's care, and I knew her only as my hostess at the interminable dinners in the cold formal villa somewhat outside of town. Later I thought of it almost as my second home, even though it was ugly and placed in the middle of a rather large formal garden and built surprisingly in the shadow of a six-floor apartment house, which I soon learned was occupied by the former wet nurse of the two Connes children. I was surprised to learn that she still worked for them and was a member of the household.

When we first went to Dijon, Marie-Clare Connes was about four and Pierre (whom Georges referred to very affectionately as *"Mon Petit Crapaud"*) was two, and I saw little of them. I was put off by what I felt was a continued proof of coldness in Madame toward the children, whom she seldom saw because of her position as the head of the English Department, which she occupied very seriously as the daughter of the great professor Emile Le Gouis of the Sorbonne.

For some reason this was always mentioned when Georges Connes's name came up, and it irked me greatly and made me feel a kind of conspiratorial friendliness toward him which was completely unconscious.

In fact, I think I was jealous of Madame Connes in a strange way, which showed itself in my constant feeling of protection toward Georges against her superiority as the daughter of the leading professor of the Sorbonne, who had married a commoner. It always seemed to me that he was laughed at by her socially.

I KNEW nothing of my other teachers but what I surmised, and what I tried not to pay any attention to, from the gossipy young ladies who exchanged French and English with me. I realize now that they counted on me for confirmation of these rumors, which they continued for almost three years to feed me, but with complete futility. I was never one to offer chitchat, much less pay any attention to it, and their hungry eyes and mouths did nothing but turn me off.

They were starved for gossip. I listened politely, though, and never gave back any information. This was my nature and it has not changed. As the young American wife of a graduate student, who in his second and third years there was named a *lecteur en Anglais,* which perforce made me a faculty wife, I was bombarded from the very first by shockingly lewd and ribald rumors about every member of the faculty, and every member of each family. It is a wonder that I could hold up my head when I faced these monsters every afternoon as one of their other students. I knew enough to curl the hair off an angel about what happened in each bedroom, and not only the connubial room but other chambers about the town, including several of the better known whorehouses.

I knew what went on with the wives too, and perforce the various children, and I cannot remember a single word of it. In one ear and out the other, was my motto, and it was not because I was prim or licentious or anything in between: I was simply uninterested in any life but my own.

I knew about Monsieur and Madame Trahard, for instance. He was the head of the department when Georges was not, and they were very good friends. Their wives were equally cordial toward each other and cold as ice to anyone else, which in this case meant me. I was a nothing to them, and very rightly so. I was at best an interruption, someone they must be polite to as their husbands' student, as well as the wife of a young Yankee assistant in the department. I continued to be afraid of Henriette Connes and bored by her, and fortunately my relations with the other wives were less dictated by my husband's position.

Monsieur Trahard was of course more brilliant than Georges Connes. I do not know what happened to him during and after the war, but he undoubtedly moved ahead in the strict order of the university life, which was controlled by the state in France. Georges chose to stay behind and ended up as the dean of the *faculté*. Like all the other professors in every university, he had served a time at first in the *lycées,* and then, after presentation of his thesis, he had moved quickly up in the ranks of the university life. The ultimate goal of every one of the products of this system was to climb upward and onward, and to end finally as department head at the Sorbonne or Strasbourg.

Some of the professors seemed more important than others, which was all dictated by the educational system so that nobody got into the university without first being a full professor at the *lycée*. There were examples always of quirks in this otherwise straightforward system. One especially was the case of Monsieur Bodin. He

was a gentleman of great prestige and built in the grand manner . . .
tall and spare and extremely noble. He had always with him the German exchange students, always female and of the upper class, to
match his own aristocratic background. He lived with a valet and
was allowed to give lectures to the university students instead of being restricted to the younger men of the *lycée.* This was because he
was fully qualified to be a full professor and at a much better university than Dijon, but he refused to finish his thesis. This refusal was
legendary in our time and may still be, in the history of the French
educational pattern. He refused to pass his thesis which would have
put him automatically on the *faculté* of some great university, and
each time his thesis was presented he would either deliberately leave
out an essential comma or put in an extra period or otherwise mar
his perfect thesis. This trick guaranteed him immunity until the next
period of examination, and he continued to lead the good life he had
chosen as a gentleman teacher in the high school of a small provincial town, unmoved by peace or war or competition or even domes-
ticity. He received what students he chose, and was a local legend as
he stalked along the streets of Dijon, always with a silver-headed
cane in one hand and his arm upon the elbow of a well-dressed German student, his "assistant."

Another freak of the university system was Jean Matrouchot.
He was a friend of Georges Connes's and also Larry Powell's, who
was known to Al and me always with some awe and no familiarity.
He was younger than Georges and was already known as an eccen-
tric, mostly because of his poor eyesight. He insisted on staying at
the *lycée* as an odd professor, and taught one or two courses and the
Cours des Vacances. And my gossips assured me that he was well-
known at the *lycée* for sometimes appearing at his eight o'clock
classes in a tuxedo. It was proof of his nightly wanderings.

One of the professors at the university was Monsieur Martenot, who had written a book used by all the foreign students called
Ne Confondez Pas . . . It was a wonderful grammar book, but I do
not know whether he was a full professor or not. Another one like
him, in that he was more important to the foreign students than to
the regular ones, was Monsieur Porteau, professor of phonetics. He
was a dark taciturn man, and he was neither popular nor unpopular

and seemed to have little to do with either the students or the professors. He was said by his wife to be drunk most of the time.

She, in turn, was the only professor's wife who fraternized with me as a student and otherwise. She was a big heavy woman, tall and dignified, and she seemed very lonely. She made something of a *confidante* of me and enjoyed having long rather tiddly teas with me, at the tea shops that served small glasses of sweet wine like marsala and sherry to the ladies of the town who did not appear often in the cafés or *brasseries*. Madame Porteau was openly friendly with me and later seized upon my sister Norah, who learned early on how to handle her liquor well. Madame Porteau befriended both Norah and me for the same vague reason; once she had been an American citizen, although she seemed more French than anyone else in the town.

The other wives of the *faculté* members were often faculty teachers themselves in *lycées*, like Madame Connes and Madame Trahard, and I seldom saw them except in their own homes in rare invitations to us students.

Probably the most fascinating of the full university professors was a thin youngish man called Jardillet. Like all the professors, he gave a course which lasted one semester and consisted of one weekly public lecture, and his were always the most popular. The grimy little amphitheater of the Faculté des Lettres was always filled to brimming over when he spoke. He was often seen around town talking with wild-eyed students over coffee in the shabbier cafés. His lectures were about politics and especially the newspaper game in France, and I followed them avidly. I was not surprised when he left the scene for Paris and a political appointment. I remember seeing pictures of him in the Pathé Newsreel, which preceded every movie in those days. There would be our own Jardillet standing just behind the president of France, or inspecting a mine in the Ruhr, or standing in the prow of a boat heading for Morocco or Algiers. All his students and his many admirers outside the university, who were mostly blue-collar, would cheer and mention him proudly. I do not know what became of him either, but suspect he died in a prison camp during the war.

There were others in the *faculté*, all of them good men in their own ways, and I took them as my due until the awful day when I saw my name with the *assez bien* printed after it in the local paper, and realized that I had never taken my classes seriously. I was damned forever. It did not matter to me as much then as it did later, but it did teach me one lesson that I never have forgotten, that knowledge gained at the university classes is something that many people live and die for, and that I was never to be in that class. I still consider it one of my great losses, and I remember with humility the many students who looked on my life as that of an honored rich person when they saw me drinking my daily *apéritif* in a warm café with my husband, or met me on the street emerging from a movie, or even a poor restaurant . . . something quite beyond their means.

There was one bright-cheeked boy from Warsaw who refused bluntly to have coffee with Al and me because he could not repay us, and when we tried to assure him that we did not expect any reciprocation and spoke vaguely of friendship, he simply shrugged and turned away in a manner that I thought was rude then, but I understand now.

There was another student I would like to have known. She appeared at all the free lectures, which occurred sometimes five afternoons a week during the winter months and were very popular. She was a Russian woman and was always seen guiding her blind father to and from their attic, to the university and home again. She was a small woman and he was even smaller, and they wore no hats but were always dressed in long big fur coats clear to the ground. They never spoke to one another or to anyone who dared to greet them and yet they were familiar to everyone, at least among the people we knew there.

She drew constantly, and once Al saw that she was drawing me during the lectures and he finally went up and asked to see what she had done. She spoke in broken French to him, and he said that she was courteous and finally showed him some very good but evil caricatures of me. He pretended to be pleased by them but really he was taken aback by their cruelty and, I think, he was glad when she refused very firmly to let him have them, even for the money he finally offered. After that, he always nodded to her when they met each other on the street, but he never spoke to her again.

I was very aware of her because she often stared at me and continued to draw me more than anybody else at the public lectures, but we never spoke and then a few months before we left, she disappeared from sight. I learned gradually that her father had died suddenly in the night, and that she had stayed there alone with his body for almost two weeks, drawing it constantly. Nobody noticed until the man's body began to smell; then she was taken away to a sanitorium, a madhouse. I never even knew her name.

It seems odd now that I remember the names of several of the students at Beaux Arts, though. Antoinette de Torcy was one. She was close to middle age and we knew her mainly through the Club Alpin, but also she dropped in now and then to toss off a few masterly watercolors at the morning classes at Beaux Arts. She was often accompanied by her friends, the Biarnoit sisters whose name was always pronounced as if it were spelled Biarnet, which meant a great deal to the name-conscious class to which they belonged, *la petite noblesse,* in their case, of Paris itself, which put them several steps ahead of the de Torcy name in Burgundy.

The younger Biarnoit sister came almost every morning to the Beaux Arts classes in watercolor and was smiled upon by the snobbish head of the school; and I became friendly with her in the same round-about way as always, to Monsieur Ollangnier's great pleasure, since his own membership in the Club Alpin had brought about this meeting of the two great cultures. In his mind's eye, I think he enjoyed our many invitations to the evenings given by Mademoiselle de Torcy and the Biarnoits even more than we did. He enjoyed hearing about them and we enjoyed going to them.

We were curiosities, that first winter especially, and we became familiars in the drawing rooms, until I could stand no more of it, and Al fortunately was easily convinced that movies improved his French more than the endless parlor games we played in the drawing rooms. We withdrew from this far from giddy scene quite naturally by the time we lost caste by moving to rue Monge; and although Al continued to read *L'Action Française* and to discuss it with the young leaders of the Royalist Movement in cafés, my own life became fuller than ever as I accustomed myself to the weekly meetings with my exchange students and all the other comings and goings at Beaux Arts and the university, the public lectures, and the movies

and my increasing absorption in writing three different accounts of
the life I led during those first years of being a ghost.

CHAPTER
NINE

AFTER CHRISTMAS the foreign students changed, at the university in Dijon. The hungry Poles with too-bright eyes, who lived through the warmer months on international fellowships and pride in unlisted attics, went back to Warsaw. The few pretty English girls who bothered to come to such a stuffy little town stopped baffling Frenchmen by their bold naiveté, and left the tea shops and the cafés for Wiltshire and Devonshire again. The cool long-limbed Swedes smelled snow, and hurried back to their own ski slopes.

Now, instead of a dozen accents in the halls of the *faculté,* you heard only one other than French, and it was German. There were Lithuanians and Danes and Czechs, but German was the tongue.

The girls all looked much alike, thick and solemn. They walked silently about the streets, reading guidebooks, in flat broad shoes and a kind of uniform of badly tailored gray-brown suits.

The men, most of them, were young and pink-cheeked and oddly eager. They sat lonesomely in the cafés, and seldom spoke to one another, as if they had been told not to. The Dijonnais students, who were still fighting the First World War, when the *sales boches* had besieged the town, were politely rude to them, and they seemed to be scattered like timid sheep, longing for a leader. It was only at the university that they dared band together, and almost before the first class of the new semester, they elected a Prussian the president, as if to prove that there at least they were united and strong.

85

I had not much to do with the student body as such; my own life with Al was too absorbing and complete, but I could not help feeling surprised to learn that Klorr was our new leader.

He was quite unlike any of the other young Germans, who seemed to dislike and almost fear him, in spite of their votes. He was as tall as they, probably, but there was something about the set of his bones that made him seem slight and weak. He wore his brownish hair rather long and slicked back against his head, not in a fair brush; and he dressed in bags and tweed jacket like an Englishman, not in a stiff short coat that showed his hips and narrow trousers, as his compatriots did.

He had a thin sneering face, too, all of a color with his pale slick hair, and it stuck forward on his neck, instead of being solid between his shoulders.

He was, I think, the most ratlike human I have ever seen, and at the same time he was tall, well set up, intelligent looking . . . a contradictory person. I dismissed him from my thoughts, as someone I would not care to know, and most surely never would.

I noticed him, though, because he and a girl distracted me several times in class before I knew who she was. I was surprised to see him with her: She was one of the big pallid ones, and I thought him the type who would marry her, finally, but spend his "student days" with someone small, light, exciting.

The two of them always seemed to be sitting right in front of me in class, and always very close together, so that her thigh pressed hard against his and her large face almost touched him. They would whisper all through the lectures. It annoyed me. I found it hard enough to keep my mind on the professorial drone about the preposition *"de"* without having to sort it out from their moist Germanic hissings.

Usually they were reading parts of letters to each other, and usually Klorr sneered coldly at the girl, who seemed to be defending what they read.

Then at the end of the class they would go silently out of the room, she carrying all his books as well as her own. Often she carried his thick topcoat, too.

I found myself interested enough in them to tell Al about them.

They seemed such a strange pair to be so intimate, and I was very naïve then about the many visages of love.

One night at supper Madame Ollangnier tore through her meal faster than ever, pushed her plate away and the dog Tango off her lap as if she had come to a great decision, and in her slowest, richest Burgundian accent asked us to make up our minds. At once, she said. There and then.

Her voice rose like a general's. Her long nose whitened. Her beautiful hard shrewd eyes, deep in wrinkles but young, looked at us with infinite enjoyment of the comedy she was playing.

"The time has arrived," she said harshly, and we wondered in a kind of stupor what joke she would tell, how soon she would burst into a great gust of laughter and release us from her teasing. We were used to her by now, but constantly fascinated, like a magician's petted nervous rabbits.

Monsieur Ollangnier stirred fussily, and popped a vigor pill under his little waxed gray moustache. "Enough," he murmured. "Enough. Don't shout so, please! My nerves tonight . . ."

She slapped, absently, fondly, at his shoulder. "Make up your minds! You Americans are all dreamers! Are you going to stay or go?"

"Go where? Why? Do you want us to go, Madame?" We were stammering, just as she planned us to, and we must have looked quite flabbergasted at the thought that we might want to leave our snug small home at the top of the house.

She shrieked, delighted with her game, and then wiped her eyes with her napkin and said softly, almost affectionately, "Calm yourselves! It's about renting the rooms. We'll have a new guest tomorrow, and if you plan to stay she shall have the good room on the street, next to Jo's. And if you . . ."

"But of course we plan to stay . . . as long as you want us."

"That's the ticket, then," she said in pure gutter-French, with a malicious grin at her husband.

And as always, as if to prove to himself or someone that he at least was a man of the world, the upper world, he murmured in his most affected way, "Charming! Charming children!"

Madame whispered to us before noon dinner the next day that

the new boarder was in the dining room. She was Czech, a ravishing beauty, daughter of a high official, someone completely sympathetic and destined to be my undying *confidante.*

Of course, it was Klorr's friend. Her name was Maritza Nankova, and she spoke when spoken to, in French somewhat better than mine was then. She was very shy for many days, but I could tell that she was lonely and envied me for being gay and happy and in love. I was almost completely uninterested in her.

She spent much of her time alone in her room when she was not at the *faculté.* Now and then we would hear her solid shoes climbing the stairs late at night, and I would feel a little ashamed of my own fullness, and think I should go pay her a visit, talk with her about her country and her family and clothes . . . things girls are supposed to talk about together.

Not long after she came, there was a minor drama going on in the Ollangnier *ménage.* We could only guess about it. Madame's voice was more hysterically high than ever, and her nose whiter in her red face; often we ate in icy silence in the little brown dining room. Finally one day Maritza was not there for noon dinner, and as if she had pulled a cork out of the situation when she went through the little door into the street, all three Ollangniers started talking at once to us. We felt flattered, of course, and somewhat dazed. Even Jo waved his delicate hands excitedly, and shook back his silky hair with dainty fire.

Madame, they all told us, had been asked by La Nankova to make a place at the table for her friend Klorr. "No, no, and again no," the two men thundered in their small ways.

"But he will pay well," Madame said. "Even filthy Boches must eat."

"Not here. Not with us. The food would choke us," they answered.

"But," she said, "La Nankova says he is very powerful, and important already in Germany . . . and what if someday he comes here the way they have come so often? Then," she went on triumphantly before they could interrupt, "then we will be glad to have a friend in him."

The enormity, the basically female realism of it, floored us all for a minute.

Then Monsieur, with a flattering little bow to me, and a slight twist of his moustache with two fingers to prove himself not only masculine but always the *boulevardier,* said, "It is bad enough, my dear, to have to see that well-behaved but clodlike peasant virgin twice a day, sitting in the same room with you and Madame Fischer. The addition of a yearning Prussian swain is more than I could bear."

Madame laughed delightedly. "Virgin, yes," she agreed shrilly. "Swain, definitely not. Klorr is much more interested in finding a good meal than exploring Maritza's possibilities. She has the appeal of a potato."

Jo flushed. "Papa is right," he said, and I thought that at last he had expressed himself, even so circumspectly, on a sexual matter. But he went on, "Mademoiselle Nankova is dull enough. No Boches, please, *Belle-mère.* "

Madame looked gently at him. He usually called her Madame. It was as if anything more intimate to this coarsely vital woman, who had taken his dead mother's place, would betray him and his father too, and he was endlessly cruel to her, the way a young person can be.

She laughed again, then, and banged on the table. "I give up," she cried. "You are all against me . . . yes, you two smug American lovers too. No Boche. If we starve, we starve together. But," and she looked maliciously at her husband, "when Paul is away on business this Klorr can eat here. My stomach is not so delicate as some, and Klorr may not be bad-looking, even if he is a German."

So she won, after all. We celebrated the ambiguous victory with a little glass of *marc* all 'round. It was the nicest lunch Al and I had eaten with them, because we felt that we were no longer well-mannered paid-up boarders, but real friends of the family. We wished Maritza would stay away oftener, or always.

The cold winter dragged into Lent. Klorr came a few times to the dining room, always when Monsieur was away, and if Jo was caught there he ate almost nothing and excused himself. The German sensed it. He was very charming to Madame, and was an entertaining talker, except for his lisp. He had a way of leaning across the table after a meal, rolling bread crumbs between his white knobby fingers, with his small strange eyes fixed almost hypnotically on his listener's.

He paid little attention to me, and none at all to Maritza, but seemed much attracted to Jo when he was there, and to Al. Al met him a few times in cafés, and told me Klorr talked mostly of the coming renaissance in Germany. Klorr said it would be based on a Uranic form of life.

I looked up the Uranism. I *think* it was Uranism. It seemed to agree with what I had seen of Klorr, at least in his attitude toward Maritza. She never spoke at the table when he was there unless he addressed her by name, and then she flushed and seemed almost to tremble. It was a strange kind of love affair, I thought.

I grew more curious about her, and determined, tomorrow or tomorrow, to see more of her, go chat with her in her room. She never looked either happy or unhappy, except now and then after a meal, when she and Madame would go into a kind of orgy of ghost stories.

Then Maritza's face would flush under her pale skin, and her large dull eyes would be full of light and almost beautiful. She would talk rapidly in her up-and-down Czech accent, and laugh and clasp her big strong hands in front of her.

Madame loved it, and sometimes matched her, tale for tale, and sometimes let her go on alone, with her strange village stories of ghouls and charms and lost cats miraculously found, and of what it meant to sneeze three times . . . that sort of thing. Maritza's eyes would stare into the steamy air, and sometimes they almost frightened me with their mute superstitious mysticism. There was the same thing about them that I have never been able to accept in some Wagnerian music, a kind of religious lewdness, maybe.

One night Al and I came through the silent streets quite late, midnight or so. We had gone to a movie and then sat drinking *café-crème* and listening to the exhausted music at the Café Miroir, hating to go out into the raw cold Dijon air.

We saw that Maritza's two windows were brightly lit, with the curtains not drawn. It was strange; always before, ever since she came, they had been dark when we unlocked the little door. We both spoke of it, and then went on tiptoe up the stairs, forgetting her for ourselves.

Much later, I opened our windows. There, across the deep silent courtyard, her inner window still shone, beside Jo's dark one. The curtains were not pulled.

It upset me a little. I stood watching for a minute, but I could see nothing. I got back into bed. I would surely go see her tomorrow, I thought . . . maybe ask her to have tea with me.

I was asleep when the knock came on the door. We both sat up sharply like startled children; it was the first time anyone had ever come to our door at night. Al clambered out, and ran on his bare brown feet to open it, with his heart probably pounding like mine, from sleep and bewilderment.

It was Jo. He stood there in a mauve woolen bathrobe, carefully not looking toward me in the bed, and asked softly, "Is Madame here? I beg her pardon a thousand times, and Monsieur Fischer's . . . but if Madame would perhaps come." He was stammering, speaking very softly with his eyes cast down.

"What's wrong?" Al asked bluntly, taking him by the arm. I don't know what he thought had happened.

"It's Mademoiselle la Nankova. She still has the light on in her room, and I can hear her. But I don't know whether she is laughing or crying. It is very soft. But it is late. I'm worried. I thought Madame Fischer, as a woman . . ."

"I'll come, Monsieur Jo," I said, and he bowed without looking at me. We heard his light steps down and up the zigzag stairs, and then the firm closing of his door on the landing across the courtyard.

Al looked upset. "Why not ask Madame Ollangnier?" he said. "I don't like your being called this way. It's cold tonight. It's . . . it's an imposition."

"You're jealous," I said, while I put his warm bathrobe over my pajamas. "You'd like to go yourself."

"To see that pudding?" he said, and we both had to laugh, even while I hurried, and his eyes blinked at me with curiosity in them as well as sleep and crossness and love.

The light was on above the top zigzag of the wide stone staircase. I went quickly, wondering what was wrong with the girl. She seemed such a dull lump. Probably she was homesick, or had cramps . . . I knocked on her door, and while I listened I could hear a little rustling in Jo's room; he was listening too, close there behind the safety of his wall. There was no sound at all in Maritza's room. I knocked again. Finally a chair was pushed back, and I heard what I thought were her firm steps across the room.

But when the lock turned and the door opened, deliberately, it was Klorr who stood there, with a white napkin held to his mouth.

I do not know what I thought: I was not embarrassed for either of us, and for some reason not surprised. We stood looking at each other, and I could see that his eyes were not pale at all, as I had thought, but very dark above the napkin. He kept patting his lips. In the room behind him I could hear Maritza breathing in long soft moaning breaths, monotonously.

I started to say why I had come, but he interrupted me in a smooth courtly flow . . . I was so kind to worry . . . just about to call me . . . our little Czech friend seemed upset . . . he had stopped for a few minutes in passing . . . undoubtedly a small indisposition that I, a sister creature, would comprehend . . . a thousand thanks, goodnight, goodnight. And he was off down the stairs, as silent and unruffled as a rat, with the napkin in his hand.

I went reluctantly inside. The room was bright with light from an enormous bulb that hung, unshaded, over the middle of the big bed. I went quickly to the curtain, and covered all the windows, like a fussy old nursemaid or like a mother protecting her daughter's modesty, for Maritza was lying there in that light, naked except for a few crumbs and grapeskins on her belly.

When I had with my instinctive gesture made things more seemly, I looked full at her.

The bed was covered with a big white sheet, as if it were a smooth table, and she motionless in the middle, lying with her arms at her sides. I was surprised at how beautiful her body was, so white and clean, with high firm breasts and a clear triangle of golden hair, like an autumn leaf. There were no pillows on the bed, so that her head tilted back and I could see pulses beating hard in her throat.

Her eyes were closed, and she kept on breathing in those low soft moans.

I leaned over her. "It's Madame Fischer, Maritza."

She did not answer or open her eyes, but at the sound of my voice she started to tremble, in long small shudders that went all over her, the way a dead snake does. I spoke again, and when I picked up one heavy arm it fell softly back. Still, I felt she knew everything that was going on.

I was not exactly puzzled . . . in fact, I seemed at the time to take the whole thing as a matter of course, almost . . . but for a minute I stood there, wondering what to do. Maritza's face was very hot, but the rest of her was cold, and shaking now with the long shuddering ripples, so I covered her with a coat from her *armoire,* after I had pushed the grapeskins and crumbs off her.

They were only on her belly. There were several crumbs down in her navel, and I blew at them, without thinking it funny at all. I put them all in my hand, and then onto a plate on the little table, before I realized how strange it was.

It was set up by the fireplace, with a linen tablecloth, and placed precisely on it were a plate of beautiful grapes with dark pink skins, an empty champagne bottle and a fine glass, and a little round cake with a piece out of it. It looked like the kind of table a butler arranges in the second act of an old-fashioned bedroom comedy, except that there was only one glass, one plate, one fork.

I knew Klorr had been supping there, while Maritza lay naked on the bed and moaned for him. And I knew that he had put the empty grapeskins on her unprotesting flesh without ever touching her.

My hands felt foul from them, I went to the *armoire,* to look for some alcohol or toilet water to rub on them, but I could see none in the neat bareness of the shelves.

I ran as silently as I could to our rooms. Al was lying in bed, reading, and when he asked me mildly what was going on, I suddenly felt a strange kind of antagonism toward him, toward all men. It was as if Maritza had been shamed in some way that only women could know about. It was as if I must protect her, because we were both females, fighting all the males.

"Nothing . . . it's all right," I said crossly. "She's got the jitters."

"Oh," Al said, and went on with his book.

I ran down the stairs with a bottle of *eau de Cologne.* I thought I would rub Maritza with it. I closed her door, and pulled the coat gently off her.

'It's Madame Fischer," I said, because her eyes were still closed.

I rubbed in long slow motions up her arms, and up her legs from her ankles, the way I remembered being massaged in a Swedish bath when I was younger. Gradually she stopped making the moan with every breath, and the unnatural shudders almost ceased. Her face was cooler, too.

"You are better, now, Maritza," I kept saying as I rubbed the toilet water into her fine white skin. "You are all right now."

It was like quieting an animal, and had the same rhythm about it, so that I don't know how long it was before I saw that the door had opened silently, and Klorr stood there watching me.

Maritza's eyes were still shut, but she felt something in my hands, although I did not feel it myself, and she began the long hard shuddering again.

Klorr was staring at me with jet-bead eyes, and hate seemed to crackle out of him in little flashes, like electricity in a cat's fur. I glared back at him. I must have looked fierce, because as I got up slowly and approached him, he backed away and out into the hall by Jo's door. He had the napkin in his hand, and he held it out to me. I closed the door into the girl's room.

"What do you want?" I asked, speaking very distinctly. I could hear my own voice, and impersonally I admired my accent. I am in a rage, a real rage, I thought, and rage is very good for the French accent.

Klorr smiled weakly at me, and wiped his lips again.

"I was just passing by," he said for the second time that night. "I . . . how is our little Czech friend? I appreciate your unusual interest in her. How is she, if I may be so bold as to inquire? Tell me, dear Madame . . . what is wrong with her?"

His smile was stronger now, and he was speaking smoothly, with his eyes staring scornfully, sneeringly at me.

Then I drew myself up. It sounds funny even to write about

now, or think about, but I actually did draw myself up, until I seemed much taller than he. And very distinctly, in the most carefully enunciated and completely pompous French that has ever been spoken outside a national theater, I said, "What is wrong with her? Mademoiselle Nankova, Monsieur Klorr, is suffering from an extreme sexual overexcitement!"

Those were my words, which sprang unsought for into my furious brain. Yes . . . they rolled out magnificently. *Une sur-ex-ci-ta-tion se-xu-el-le* . . . syllable by mighty syllable, even to the final "le," like a quotation from Racine.

Klorr looked away. He bowed stiffly, and then as if he could not stand it any longer he threw the napkin at me and ran again down the stairs, as silent as a rat.

When I went back into the room, Maritza was curled up like a child in the middle of the bed, crying peacefully into her hands. She was rosy and warm, and I put the coat over her and turned out the light and went home. I felt terribly tired.

Al was asleep. He never asked me anything about it, and I never told him.

The next day Maritza was the same as always, shy and dull as if she did not know me, and in about a week she left, without saying goodbye to any of us. Madame said that she and Klorr, by a very odd coincidence, were going to be in Venice together for the Easter celebrations.

"Love is hair-raising," Madame said. "Imagine that great lump in a gondola."

"I for one am thankful," Monsieur said, rolling his eyes first toward the good God in heaven and then toward me. "Now we can resume our old chats, without having to wait for La Nankova to keep up with us, and without having to escape her questionable Prussian acquaintance. It will be excellent for practice, for perfecting the accent."

Monsieur Jo looked at me, and before he lowered his soft eyes in their deep curling lashes, he smiled in an abashed way at me, and murmured, "But Madame's accent is already excellent at times, Papa."

And I burst out laughing, and could tell nobody why. Whenever

I say those words in my mind, I must laugh now, in spite of the feminine shame I feel to think of that table laid in the bright room, and of the strange ways of satisfying hunger.

(I do not know now why I think this dream I had the next morning should be here. It is something about Al's brown feet, I think . . . but it does show how intimately my three written lives were woven into the waking pattern. It was written the morning after the incident with La Nankova and Klorr, sometime in April of 1930. Of course, I never showed this to Al, but I do know that neither of us had ever met the Count in real life, although he was completely familiar to me in the dream.)

NIGHT IN A FRENCH TOWN

That quick knock on the bedroom door cut like a cry across the soft rushing of the night rain, and made the blood leap in our veins.

"Who is there?" Al called.

His voice was clean-edged, and as I reached automatically toward the bottom of the bed for my bathrobe, I thought with a kind of pride that neither of us acted like people awake for only a few seconds. He touched my arm.

"Wait.

"Who is there?" And he raised his voice a little, although we both seemed to know that no answer would come. Only the rain drummed on against the roofs and the round cobbles, something malignant now in its insistent quiet.

I remember that as I followed him across the cold floor I noticed that he had no slippers on. It was silly, I thought. Why were we out of bed at all, out of bed in the wet air of two in the morning, for a dreamed noise? But Al had heard it too. Did we love each other so much that we dreamed together?

We went on through the black room, walking swiftly on tiptoe. Just as my hand touched the doorknob, Al snapped on the light, and we stood squinting at each other in the bright glare. He looked full at me, his eyes slowly widening, telling me what I could not understand, nor he neither, and then I opened the door.

It was the Count, stooping in the low attic corridor. He wore a brown beard, with rain in it. I thought he was in Africa.

Al didn't know him, but held open the door silently, as if he had long expected this night visit, and the Count stepped inside the room and leaned against the wall, breathing with soft, rapid sounds, worse than curses or loud moaning. His face wore the old detached, rather supercilious look, more than ever like a smooth mask, with the rain on it.

He took Al's left hand quickly in one of his, and then mine in his other, and we stood quite still for several heartbeats. I heard five, I remember, with the rain touching the roof in separated drops between each one of them. Everything was very distinct. I could feel Al's hand in the Count's as well as I could feel my own . . . the infinite rustle of live skin against live skin, and the slight jarring of small delicate joints as they moved with our spirits in that strange compact. Then we fell apart, and the Count said in a low, breathless voice, as if he were going to cough, "Pull the curtain. I must not be seen."

He leaned back against the wall again, looking down at us over his high browned cheekbones as Al pulled the thick curtain quickly across the window and I stood wondering why I felt so impassive. I saw with no surprise, as if I had already known it for a long time, that the Count made Al and me look immature, that he was very long and bony, that his eyes were not the brown childlike ones in which I had once put much trust. That made me vaguely sorrowful.

Now he looked quickly at us, at our room, at the window, with eyes half-closed and hotly pained . . . and rather fearful. I thought of a sick man waiting for the confessional to empty, and of a Negro I had once seen walking down the street the day after his cousin was lynched for rape.

"I thought you were a doctor in Africa, Count."

"I am in great danger," he said, as if he had not heard me, or did not want to. "Yes, great danger. But here for tonight I shall be quite safe."

He jerked back his head in a grimace of amusement, and Al and I smiled too, foolishly.

"Count, you're soaked. You're shivering," I said. "Take off your coat and sit down."

"No, no. No thanks."

He was looking around the room again.

"Where does that door go?"

"To the workroom. Take off your shoes, anyway, and put on Al's woolly slippers." I was worried. He looked as if he were going to faint.

"No. I'll go in there."

"You can't, Count. It's cold as hell in there, and the skylight's leaked all over the floor. Anyway, there's clay all over everything. You can't go in there, Count."

He looked past me and walked towards the door on the balls of his feet. He was almost in the room. Suddenly he backed out, his eyes nearly shut, and spoke to Al.

"Will you please put a curtain or cloth over the skylight?" he asked in his queer, shut voice, which sounded more than ever like the instant before a cough.

Al went into the big drafty room. I heard him stumble over a box or some other hollow wooden thing, and pull the squeaking cord for the light-curtain, before he turned on the one small electric bulb that dangled from the middle of the damp ceiling. Then the Count went in, and I after him.

Al came over beside me, and we stood looking at the Count as he walked under the light. For some reason I suddenly wondered if he were bleeding to death, although I had no idea of what he should look like in that case. He turned to us, with his head thrown back perhaps for air, and his eyes, half-closed, regarding us over his cheekbones as if we really weren't there.

"Thank you. This is very nice. It will do well for tonight," he said gently. "Now go back to bed. And in the morning we shall see."

What shall we see? I knew Al wondered too . . . or perhaps things were already clear to him.

The Count jerked his head again in a gesture of strange amuse-

98

ment, and this time without smiling in return, Al and I went toward the door.

As I closed it after us, I saw him standing with his arms in two lines along his tall body, his head still back in the echo of that soundless laughter. Light fell upon his shoulders, and sparkled in the raindrops on his great beard, but darkness waited like a sea, all around him.

While I stood with my hand still holding the cold knob of the workroom door, I watched Al go across the floor to the electric-light button. He looked very young in his wrinkled white pajamas, with his hair curling up in brown twists into the air. His feet were more than ever like those of a young monk, long, slender, delicate, with muscles moving in smooth ridges under the brown skin. I recognized at that moment, seeing him there so young, a sadness that had always been in me, waiting, and would never again go back to its hiding-place. It rose with an inevitable surging in my throat, over my heart, and up into my head. No wailing now, but I touched the wall behind me.

The light snapped out. Al came swiftly to my side, and pulled back the heavy faded curtain, and suddenly the room was filled with the insistent beating of the rain on the roofs and the small round stones and the hard floor of the courtyard. We stood close together, and looked out over the black well of the court, over the wall and the little garden next door and its high iron grill with points on it, and into the street. There the rain fell down in bright streaks around the leaning gas lamp in its shining glass box. We could see a few feet up and down the gleaming sidewalk, then the hard black sides of other houses cut into its faint powdery light. It looked resolute all alone.

Al kissed me on the mouth, and we went back to bed.

At first it seemed quite right to be warm again. We lay without talking, as if exhausted, breathing slowly. Then I realized that Al hadn't spoken to me for a long time, not since the knock on the door. At that sudden knowledge I stiffened, and lay sickly, while over me swooped in a dark winging all the weird sounds and pictures of the night, with Al's silence the meaning of every one of them: A dark thread knitting darker happenings together. It was impossible! I started fiercely to speak to him, to ask him why. Then I heard his slow breathing, deep and tired. No, don't wake him.

I waited a long time, with open eyes, while the strange sadness of that night pushed on and on in me, filling my bones and flooding my brain and all the inner twistings of me, until I wondered that I did not burst and die. Al breathed beside me, and the rain fell down, and in the workroom the Count walked slowly over the small cluttered space, with shuffling sounds. His steps and the rain and Al's slow breaths marked with an unchanging rhythm the tide's flowing, while I lay listening, waiting for the ebb.

I sat up.

Only the quiet rushing of the rain now made the night sound. The Count had stopped pacing. Al's long breaths had ceased, and when I looked over at him I could see by two darker spots on his dark head that his eyes were open. He sat up too, and as if someone were calling us we got up silently and went to the window.

It was raining harder now, and a colder wind blew in on us, but we stood there close together for a long time . . . perhaps even half an hour . . . watching the man in the street.

He stood as the Count had stood in the workroom, with light from the steady gas lamp falling on his shoulders and down the straight lines of his hanging arms. His head was thrown back, but we could see that he was not smiling. Everything in him was drawn into his eyes, which looked up at our house with an intensity that I have never seen before or after those minutes. He seemed to be in a trance, to be turning his whole self into a pair of eyes that could look through cloth and wood and stone, and over walls and around corners.

He was naked except for a black cloth around his loins, and the rain made his dark skin gleam and shine like armor over the wide shoulders and thick chest and the short, taut arms and legs. He was beautiful: an Annamite or Chinese broadsword champion without his clothes, I thought.

And the slight bamboo stick in his hand was a blowpipe. That seemed quite natural, too.

As Al and I stood looking at him, watching with the nonchalant attention of two minor actors in a long-run play, a little creature came into the patch of street. It swung lightly along the edge of the sidewalk, and up on the shoulder of the man, who held out one arm to it without turning his eyes away from the house. At first we thought it was a monkey, with its long hanging arms, thin as sticks, and its little black spider-body. But when it jumped high up under the light, sitting easily on the man's shoulder, with one hand in his wet hair, it seemed more human . . . a little boy, incredibly thin and agile, or perhaps a tiny dwarf from some jungle filled with monkeys.

It leaned its small round head close to the man's ear. For the first time he lowered his eyes . . . (beside me Al sighed with relief) . . . while the little black monkey-boy made gestures with his arms, and moved his wide thin lips. No sound came to us from that queer monologue, but we knew the man was hearing necessary things. He stood immobile under the light, one arm crooked up to his companion, the other holding at his side the blowpipe, his head bent . . . and all his body listening.

I leaned forward, hypnotized by his attention, trying to hear words I would not understand. The man threw back his head, his face stretched with pleasure, and looked straight into my eyes. I gasped. I drew back, shocked, filled with terror and revulsion. Al stood silently beside me. I heard a movement in the workroom, and suddenly realized that the rain was slowing off, falling less fiercely on the town: ebbing.

When I looked again, the little creature was down in the gutter, with gold water around his fragile legs. He looked up at the man, who nodded. Then in three flying bounds, like a spider jerked from above on his invisible thread, he lit on the top of the iron garden grill. He waved his tiny black hand.

The man thrust the bamboo tube into his loincloth, breathed until his chest bulged out and all his ribs raised themselves against the tight skin, and glided across the wet cobbles.

He disappeared for a second. Then his head showed between the black bars of the grill. He drew himself lightly up to the top.

The two stood there, looking up at our window. Then, the monkey-boy first, the man after him, they advanced like two tight-rope dancers across the narrow iron bar, curving their bare feet delicately between the golden spikes that pointed up along its hard ridge.

It was easy to jump the few feet up to the smooth broad top of the garden wall.

They stopped there a minute, looking down into the dark well of the courtyard, bottomless in the night. They were silhouetted against the wall across the street by the clear gaslight, which gleamed up through the slowing rain.

We could see the thin, twisted outlines of the little creature, bent down like an old root against the man's leg. The other, thick and short, stood, black as the well into which he looked, and drew himself slowly together. It was like watching a cat prepare to leap from a high shelf. He did not stir, but every fiber in his body held itself ready under the still skin. He breathed out his great ribs. The little boy crouched below him, in a hunched knot.

They jumped.

I have never seen bodies fall as slowly as theirs. They drifted down, arms waving languidly. Before they went out of our sight into the depths of the court, I thought they would surely turn over. It was as if we were seeing the whole thing at slow speed, and would soon reverse the order and see them float gently back to the top of the wall.

Nothing happened. They disappeared. No sound came to us, no thud of flesh on stone, no wet noise of disturbed puddle. They lit as silently as snow.

Outside the window no rain fell now to make the night stir with sound. The quiet became heavy and merciless, a weight pressing over our breasts, stopping our nostrils and filling our ears with the surge of excited heart-blood.

A drop of water fell at regular intervals into a drain. It was like a clock, ticking off new time in a new space.

Al turned on the light. He walked stiffly back to me. I looked once more at his long supple feet, skeleton feet with brown silk skin. His hands were like that, too, the thumbs broad and strong.

The sadness and the pity of all this still filled me, but now I knew that nothing could help. It was too late . . . too late even to be sorry.

We stood side by side, waiting.

There were four flights of stairs for them to climb, two of yellow stone, then two of grey wood, all worn with twenty decades of marching, stamping, stumbling, noisy feet. But their feet made no sound.

We knew the steps, eleven to each flight. We knew how long it took to mount them: one at a time with tiredness or politeness, two at a time for fun, three at a time if one of us was coming to the other. At two at a time, they ought to be at the first wooden stairs, although not for fun. But they didn't walk, so how could we know? They seemed to be flowing up to our door, or floating. All we knew was that they were coming.

Why doesn't Al say something, I wondered.

Why don't they come, and finish things?

The door opened, slowly, noiselessly. I don't think even the handle turned. No, it didn't.

The man stood with wide eyes in the sudden light, eyes long and quite empty of anything except a burning, consuming search. His brown face and all his brown gleaming body leaned forward, as if nothing could hold him now from his goal. The monkey-boy crouched lightly on his shoulder.

They looked slowly at me. I never thought to turn away. Their eyes, his fierce and vacant, the little boy's glittering with a mounting pleasure, slid carefully up my body, stopped at my beating throat, then jumped. They leaped in their sockets, and seemed to pounce on Al. They fastened there, on his white covered chest.

The man felt in his cloth, and drew out the blowpipe. He looked always at Al. His hand moved very carefully.

Al sighed. All the air in him seemed leaking out between his lips.

The man put the pipe to his lips.

Then the workroom door slammed violently open. And the Count stood there, a black loincloth around his naked body.

(And that is all I remembered the next day, or until I found the story many years later. And it seemed odd that there was no broken glass along the high wall between the Archbishop's garden and our court-yard.

I was puzzled then and I continue to be even now, by my apparent knowledge of the Count. I have no idea where he came from really, nor what would have happened to any of us if the dream had gone on. But it was hardly meant to end with the usual banality of any of us living happily ever after, although some of us did.)

CHAPTER

TEN

MONSIEUR OLLANGNIER always resented having paying strangers at his table, but had little to say about it in the face of his wife's pecuniary delight in them, and he only put his foot down, and then lightly, about Germans.

So there were a few who ate with us now and then. They never stayed long. Paul Ollangnier really won, because he was so loathsomely, so suavely polite, so overpoweringly the tight-lipped French courtier, that the poor baby-Boches soon found other places to eat. Madame grinned affectionately and rather proudly, and soon refilled the empty chairs with pretty Romanian girls, or large heavy Czechs.

She liked to have at least one safely attractive female at the table; it kept Paul's small pretentious mind off his various aches and grouses, and made it easier for her to continue her own robust and often ribald life. I did very well . . . I was young and amusing, and at the same time safely and obviously in love with my husband. Monsieur Ollangnier made himself truly charming to me, and even Jo, now and then, would flutter from his sexless dreamworld long enough to make a timid joke with me. It was good for my French, and pleased Madame. Life would have been hell if it hadn't.

There was one young man who came about once a month, to take examinations at the College of Pharmacy. He was personable, but very serious about his promising future as chief chemist of a pharmaceutical firm in Lyon, after he passed his finals and then took his required military service. He paid little attention to me, but was politely attracted to Al, at least enough to cause rather impolite cackles from Madame Ollangnier.

There were also often young Romanian girls. They all followed a set pattern of behavior. And one whom I remember in particular was a pretty girl who talked too much about money and was proud of having learned to chew gum from an American boy who was enamored of her one time in Romania. She had many friends who gave her presents . . . and taught her things, too, no doubt. As Madame Ollangnier said, "Her eyes are sticky as honey . . . but men should learn to disentangle themselves before morning."

Her friends, one at a time, of course, found that morning came too soon, and after serving breakfast to several of them, Madame revolted, saying that she had been in almost every profession but that of running a brothel and wasn't yet ugly enough to start.

And at least a few times there was a Japanese student. He was a silent man and he ate very slowly, as if he were slowly and politely consuming wormwood or ashes. His face wore always the same quiet look of inward distaste, and his gestures spoke always with a voice restrained, contemptuous, and distantly kind. He called himself Monsieur Moti, and with no reason at all I had a feeling of certainty that he was lying.

He had come with perfect assurance into the French family. Madame had said one day, "Tomorrow noon we shall have a new *pensionnaire,* a Japanese."

Monsieur looked up from his plate with a frown. "A Japanese? But I have said that I don't want you to let that race come here. It is bad enough to be surrounded. . . ." He wanted to say, ". . . with spying Germans and rich Americans," but he stopped politely and scowled at his wife.

"Yes, I know," she answered, "but this boy is all right."

She had reason to say that with such confidence, for we saw at once that our new companion was a person complete in himself. With him there was no need of chatter, no protecting laugh or foolish gape of assumed interest to hide nostalgia and its accompanying woes. For him the French language was something to be absorbed as a machine absorbs oil or an infant milk. He made no effort to talk, no effort to improve his stiff and monotonous accent, with which he made one or two remarks each meal in his courteous, detached way. (He went with Al to the cafés now and then and Al was amazed to learn he never sat with his haunches touching the seat like other men, but instead, because of his muscular control, always sat two inches in the air. It was an impossible feat, of which he boasted quite casually.

And then there was, of course, Lawrence Clark Powell, who came down to Dijon from Paris in the spring of 1930. It seemed quite natural that he would come there for absolutely no valid reason that I can think of, except that he had been a senior at Occidental College when I was doing my one year there as a sophomore. He was very important in every way, and he was almost professionally the campus Bad Boy, often demoted from his high position in his fraternity, or even expelled from school, for drunkenness and general obstreperous behavior.

Of course, at Occidental he did not know me from Eve, but I remember being impressed by his *maîtrise* at the piano. He played like an angel and had a weird trick of ending his solo adaptations of everything from Brahms to "Onward Christian Soldiers" by hitting one false note at the end very deliberately, with a strange sideways leer at the audience. It always made us laugh. Everyone laughed from the president on down to the freshman nymphettes.

I knew more about him than most people did because he was in love with Faye Shoemaker, who was in turn the best friend and roommate of my sister Anne, once I finished my sophomore year and left school to marry Al.

Larry graduated with his usual bravado and tumultuous flair for publicity of every kind, and he and Faye lived together the following year while he worked at Jake Zeitlin's bookstore in Los Angeles. They parted by the end of that year and he went with his mother to England, as I learned from my sister. And then suddenly, he appeared in Dijon, most probably because of what Anne herself had decided about my life there in that strange town.

Larry was soon installed in the room next to Monsieur Jo's, where I had last been the night of the Czech girl Maritza's sexual orgy or whatever it was, and we started a fine relationship, which is still one of the best of my life.

Al and Larry immediately became true friends and my feelings toward them both were firmly set from the beginning. As I remember, we used to buy a bottle of wine now and then at the little Spanish wine shop nearby, and Larry and Al and I would go up to Larry's room or to our little purple-lavender-brown rooms. We had an old phonograph, and we'd play records and talk about affairs and drink a bottle of Moulin à Vent 1928, which cost something like a dollar then. We lived it up that way, but I was always the third wheel, always agreeing, always listening and smiling.

I remember once I disagreed during one of our many evenings in Larry's room. Larry announced firmly that he was going to learn to be a writer, and suddenly I found myself disagreeing completely with him. I said something very firm about the impossibility of becoming anything but an accomplished author, because writers were born, and that no matter how much study and skill went into the training of a man, he would never "become" a writer. Both Larry and Al disagreed with me firmly and even somewhat scornfully. Al was already convinced that he was a writer, which I think indeed he was, and Larry believed that he could become one, and by now he is considered so by many people. I soon shut up, and never again voiced any strong opinion to either of these men, although I still believe what I tried so fiercely to say that one night. As far as I know it was never referred to again. We continued as long as we were together to eat and drink and talk amiably, thankfully, and freely, except on this one subject. And I am fortunate indeed that Larry and I are still alive and are still as good friends as we have always been.

It is perhaps odd that he became estranged from Al after some ten years of open devotion. I think that Larry still thinks of him as a dear friend, but I doubt that Al was capable of carrying on a relationship for so long. It was fine indeed, though, while it lasted and it was especially good during the two years we were together in France.

Larry finished his thesis on Robinson Jeffers after we left Dijon, but our paths have crossed often since then, and always with real pleasure. This is something that can seldom be said.

He was a small man with hunched over shoulders and long boney white hands with the enlarged knuckles of a professional pianist. We ate together for much more than a year at the Ollangnier's and the Rigoulot's, and then when we moved to rue Monge he and his mother lived in our little apartment on the rue du Petit-Potet. His mother was very important to Larry, and I saw more of her than I did most people there. She was small like Larry, with large drowned eyes, and the somewhat wispy manner of a highly sensitive female whose husband had died and left her very rich, with stocks and bonds that soon became worthless. She was deeply involved in astrology and was very much troubled by what she read in my stars and Al's.

This open embarrassment was made painfully clear to me several years later when I learned through Larry that she had seen much more financial and worldly success in my horoscope than in Al's. But she did not feel that a man should know that his wife was destined to be ahead of him in the world, which explains some of her strange behavior toward me, during the months when she was living in Dijon and I was supposed to enjoy having afternoon tea often with with her, and otherwise behaving like a correctly raised young American girl with a woman of her own class. I felt much older than she ever could feel, and was ill at ease when I tried to play my role.

Larry's friend Harry Ward Ritchie, who dropped the Harry when he was in Paris studying fine printing with the great Schmied, came down to Dijon often to see us, and he became a very good close friend to us both. His mother visited with Larry's mother in Dijon, and I found myself cast forever in the role of the obedient younger woman trying to trot around with two elderly ladies, ordering their tea for them, and making the proper correct small talk; I ended by much preferring Larry's mother, although I realized then that neither they nor I had anything in common, and that my own mother was in a class quite apart from them.

After his mother left, we saw Ward more often, and I remember once that he stopped on his way up from Spain where he had stayed with Robert Bridges. He was almost unbearably smelly, because of a suit of purported tweed that he had bought in Majorca for four dollars, and which he wore proudly for a long time in spite of the insults of people like us. He survived both the suit and the insults with his own strange aplomb, a mixture of seeming shyness and impervious hard cold craftiness.

I was glad that Larry and his mother could stay in our apartment. I seldom saw her during the last months of our three years in Dijon, but I'm very glad that I met her, and that she could be there with Larry, who loved her very dearly.

Among the other occasional boarders, there was Miss Lyse, but she was in a special class . . . she was not a student. She was a type. She knew it and wore all the usual symbols proudly. She fitted every description ever written of exactly what she was, a small proud representative of every Miss Lyse in every town and city of the Western World.

She was about eighty then, I think, with a small pyramid of a body, and a fine proud little head with dark eyes and ivory skin inherited from her Portuguese father. Her features were fine and almost beautiful, with dark merry eyes, and daintily flushed cheeks, and her white hair curled just enough to look almost girlish, swept into an old-fashioned pompadour that accentuated her aristocratic rather stiff posture.

She had lived in Dijon since she was a girl, teaching English to the upper-class families there. She had been a teacher ever since her militantly British mother had brought her there, some sixty years before. She would be one until she died, helped always and in spite of her dwindling powers of instruction by the impatiently thoughtful families whose parents and grandparents had recited the verb *to be* at her virginal knee.

She still knew some English, all of it in simple words for the children she was used to talking to, but it was plain that French was more comfortable for her. She spoke it with a rank British accent, and in spite of all the decades she had spent in the nurseries and drawing rooms of Burgundy, she sounded like a schoolgirl on a month's holiday from London, except for her volubility.

For years now, since her tyrannical dam breathed one last command and folded her hands in the death-grip over her cut jet locket, Miss Lyse had been cadging meals. She did it charmingly, amusingly.

She knew everybody, and all of the provincial gossip. She went to all the weddings of her former pupils, and then the christenings and the weddings of their children . . . and when the season was slack, and they remembered, they sent baskets of wine and cakes and butter to her attic room, as if in apology for the lack of festivals.

She was a character, everyone in Dijon said. She had followed the Bishop up the bloody steps of Saint Jacques, during the great troubles between church and state, and had been stoned for it. Sadi Carnot had lain dying in her arms, assassinated. She had been a child in India where her father was ambassador and she knew how to charm snakes. That was the way the Dijonnais felt about her. She was also considered socially acceptable by Monsieur Ollangnier, who felt he was pulling off something of a coup by offering her a full lunch once or twice every month. She appealed to his snobbish nature because she knew everyone in Dijon society, and he was in various ways a snob.

Myself, I was more than interested; there was something so indomitable about the set of her head and the fine flash of her old, old eyes.

She had been Miss Lyse for at least fifty years when Al and I first met her. She came regularly for dinner every other Saturday, and we always ate better than usual on her days. Monsieur Ollangnier was especially courtly to her and he made it clear to all of us that we must always refer to her as Miss Lyse, and never "Miss" alone, as if she were an ordinary English governess or nanny. Monsieur Jo kissed her hand with a special dash, and soon Al too was under her spell. Madame and I stayed comparatively silent during her days.

It was easy to see that she had once been very lovely. Her small dark-eyed head rose above its lumpy old body like the dream of a swan, or a piece of Chinese crystal.

It was hard to see why she had not long since married some member of the aristocratic families with whom she lived; hard, that is, until you heard her describe—so lovingly, too—her genteel Tartar of a mother, who on her deathbed had made Miss Lyse swear, never, *never* to forget her English accent. And now, with this old maid who for more than half a century had spent all her days with the fine flower of Burgundy, her soft flat voice was as British as a

currant bun; her intonation so carefully preserved marked her anywhere as a "Miss," never a Fräulein or a mamzelle, and her French
was half English, her English very French.

She was garrulous, with the embarrassingly naive language of
an aged person who has spent all her life explaining things simply to
children, who might have listened better had the explanations been
complex.

She talked with a vivacity which had long since ceased to be affected, and was now as much a part of her as her jet brooch of the
young Queen Victoria, or her lace fichu that had been admired (on
another's shoulder) by Franz Joseph.

"Once, my dears," she told us on a chill October afternoon
when even shawls laid along the window-ledges could not keep cold
drafts from shushing into her high attic room, "once I stood so close
to the great Sadi Carnot that to touch him I would have been able!
Yes, then I was that near!

"That was the summer after we went near Vézelay to the country house of my little pupils—you remember?"

She peered merrily at us, and we nodded recognition to a season dead some forty years before we were conceived. We poured
another glass of sherry for her, the sherry we had brought to warm
her bones while we were far from her and the Côte-d'Or.

(And here it is perhaps significant to say that all old pupils
treated Miss Lyse thus, feeling a kind of guilty neglect if they did not
often go to her stuffy pleasant garret with wine, a cold chicken, even
a pat of sweet butter. I am sure that we kept her alive for years in this
compulsive, desultory way—)

"Yes, that was *such* a nice summer! The trees in full bloom
early were, and everybody said that *never* had there been so many
forest flowers. I remember the *Count* himself said that to me, one
morning on the stairs!"

She coloured delicately, and raised her young dark eyes above
the rim of her glass. "I used to wear flowers in my hair—it was black
then—except at dinner, of course, when I was invited down to dine
with the family if they needed an extra one at table.

"But there was one thing about that summer—when was it, in
'sixty-eight?" She looked sharply at our blank faces, as if she had a

114

good mind to rap our knuckles for inattention, and then laughed. "What does it matter? It was several years ago, yes? A beautiful summer.

"My dear blessed mother was with me, in the village near the *Château*—I had not been long away from England, and she watched over me—and one day, one day we had a picnic, a real English tea in the forest! It was lovely! My mother, and a sweet young Russian girl who taught also at the *Château,* and—"

Suddenly she put down her glass, giggled, and peeked naughtily at us between her knobby, loose-skinned fingers.

"Now you must never tell, never!" She looked stern for a second, and then giggled again. "It was very daring, but my dear mother was there and Tanya, and—three—young—gentlemen—from—the *Château!*

"Yes, my dears! We all went on the picnic, Tanya and the three young gentlemen (so handsome were they), and myself, and of course my dear good mamma to see that everything was proper.

"*Well,*" and she settled herself back in her chair as we filled her glass again, "we went far into the woods, with a servant to carry the tea-basket. We came to a stream, such a small sweet brooklet was it, with flowers and watercress on its borders.

"My mother sat down, and whilst the servant built a little blaze, she got out her silver teapot, which had gone to India twelve times with her. It was a pretty teapot.

"We gathered watercress. One of the young gentlemen—what *was* his name, now?—got his gloves quite wet. They were pale yellow gloves, of the thinnest kid, and from *Paris,* too.

"Then my dear mamma boiled water from the little brook, the most sparkling water I have ever seen, and when it just began to bubble she poured it over the tea, and then we drank. And, my dears, I never, *never* have such tea tasted!"

Miss Lyse looked at us almost somberly. We felt very young and serious as we watched her raise her glass slowly to her lips and then set it down again.

"No, it was tea like no tea before—or since. I have often boiled the water from brooklets, and poured it over the same brand of tea, *and* in my dear mother's silver teapot that to India twelve times went. But that tea, that summer afternoon near Vézelay, with dear mamma and Tanya and the three young gentlemen—and the little flowers, and I remember the poor yellow gloves—"

Miss Lyse was silent. She sipped slowly, and her eyes looked far back, like the picture of Albrecht Dürer's mother.

"Thank God in heaven," she concluded, emphatically, "that my poor departed mother watched over me, or I should not be where I am! That tea, so clear, so piquant like fine white wine from Chablis. . . ."

CHAPTER

ELEVEN

WHEN THE Rigoulots bought the house on the rue du Petit-Potet from the Ollangniers, they took us along with the stuffed deer heads and empty *Souvenirs de Verdun*. We stayed on in our little mustard-and-purple rooms, crammed by now with our own bookish castings, and we ate in the same stuffy spotted dining room. And Larry Powell stayed on in the big beautiful room that Maritza had had, next to Monsieur Jo's, in the front part of the house. Our new friends the Rigoulots were as extravagantly lavish as the others had been penny-pinching, and we tasted some of the headiest dishes of our lives there.

The Rigoulots were on their last legs as people, really. She was trying desperately to keep them together. While we were all living in this shabby house that was supposed to be good because it was on a good street just behind the Faculté des Lettres of the university, Madame Rigoulot's parents were living in elegance on the ground floor of a lovely old town house in a beautiful quarter of Dijon.

Madame Rigoulot bought the house from the Ollangniers with the last bit of her dowry, in an attempt to save their lives. She really knew absolutely nothing about providing. She was an amateur, and we lived like the rest of the family on a path of destruction, eating and drinking away in the small dining room.

We were the first boarders the family had ever had, and I am sure that we ate and drank much more every month than we paid for. There was nothing to do about it; the family was on the brink of

119

complete financial ruin, after twenty years of living on Madame's enormous but now vanished *dot,* and even if we had tried to eat one less slice of brandy-cake, one bowl less of hot creamy soup, the Rigoulots would have gone on, bilious and gay, buying fine legs of lamb and casks of wine and baskets of the most expensive vegetables.

Madame herself did the cooking, helped by a series of numb orphan slaveys, and even in the better days, when she had commanded her own small staff of servants, I think she probably kept one foot in the kitchen. She was the daughter of the finest *confiseur-pâtissier* in Alsace, a spoiled stuffed daughter who when her husband's penchant for provincial backstage beauties drained the last francs from her fabulous *dot* dropped all her elegant . . .

It is strange . . . or perhaps it is natural . . . that I cannot go on as I had planned.

I meant to write about what I learned, my gastronomic progression there with the Rigoulots . . . and even if I'd willed it otherwise there would have been some of that progression, close as I was to people who knew flavors as their American counterparts knew baseball batting averages, whether they were twelve like Doudouce or seventy-five like Papazi.

But now when I think of the hot quarrelsome laughing meals: the Sunday dinners in the formal *salle à manger* and the enormous suppers so soon afterward, when Papazi produced his weekly triumph of a tart as big as a cartwheel, with all the apple slices lying back to belly to back in whorls and swoops; the countless birthdays and name days and saint's days with their champagne and their truffled geese; the ordinary weekday suppers, "light" after the heavy meal at noon, when *soufflés* sighed voluptuously at the first prick, and cold meats and salads and chilled fruits in wine and cream waited for us . . . no, when I think of all that, it is the people I see. My mind is filled with wonderment at them as they were then, and with dread and a deep wish that they are now past hunger. They were so unthinking, so generous, so stupid.

Monsieur and Madame Emile Bonamour, or Papazi and Mamazi, the grandparents, lived in another house, a lovely place with chestnut trees in the courtyard and thin-legged gold chairs in the darkened drawing room, but their hearts were still in Alsace in the fine bright days of wealth, when Papazi was known everywhere for his chocolates and his wedding cakes.

Mamazi was a small bewigged woman, still weeping for her son lost in the first war, and meekly waspish. She shook like an idling ocean liner from all the digitalis she took, and died a little while after I saw her last. Papazi hobnobbed like an exiled king with the better of the Dijon *confiseurs,* and listened to Beethoven concerts on his TSF radio, and every week or so baffled his grandchildren with a deft masterpiece for Sunday supper or for fun. He was a merry old man, in spite of his pomposities.

The second spring when the Rigoulots were there, we were worked subtly and completely into a frenzy for snails by Papazi's sure suggestion. As soon as burgeons darkened the bare branches he began speculating mildly on the possible time for the annual snail hunt.

The weeks went by and leaves burst out on all the trees, and Papazi brought little twigs to the table and rubbed them between his thick dexterous fingers.

"Quite crisp," he would remark, ruminatively. "Yes, I really do think, in fact I am almost sure, that the snails this year will be finer, sweeter, plumper, truly more delicious than ever before."

He looked calmly at his delighted listeners.

The children were almost beside themselves.

"When can we go, Papazi? How about next Sunday? How about tomorrow? Will we get enough?"

"Calm yourselves, my dears! This excitement will ruin the taste of your mother's delicious *quenelles!* "

Plume and Doudouce subsided like pricked popovers, and Dédé smacked his lips more loudly than ever over a fresh bite, to show his mature appreciation. Papazi ate silently for a minute.

"No, not next Sunday," he continued finally. "Not next Sunday, but perhaps the Sunday after. That is," he added, hastily, before the children could open their mouths to shout great glee, "*if* the snails have fed well enough, and *if* there are not too many noxious weeds for them to ruin themselves on, this year! And of course, after we have gathered them, something may happen to spoil them. It is a long and difficult business, the preparing of snails!"

The first time I heard Papazi say this I was fool enough to ask, "Why not buy them, then, all ready to eat?"

There was a shocked silence. The children stared at me. Papazi grew pink and haughty. Finally his daughter rebuked me, very gently:

"Oh, but Madame! Nobody can prepare snails like Papazi. These store snails are good, yes—but to fix them as my father does is an art! It is an achievement!"

I never acted so thoughtlessly again, but we were glad when the hunting-time came to end, we hoped, the daily speculations.

That nightfall we returned from the woods, with most of our snails unescaped from the sacks we carried them in. It had been a pleasant day.

The next morning we noticed a large packing-box in the court-yard. It was covered with a sheet of glass, and on the glass were glued the bottoms of what seemed a thousand snails, warming themselves upside down.

At night it was still there, and the next day.

"They must purify themselves," Papazi explained. "They must get rid of any poisonous food in them. They must, you might say, starve to death!"

"How long will it be, then?"

"A few days—a week, perhaps: These are very sturdy snails."

Indeed they were. For a day or two more they stayed, bottoms up, on the glass. Then they began to drop off. Nights were punctuated by the thumps of snails fainting in their little Black Hole. We lost sleep, feeling very sick for them, waiting for the hunger swoon to overcome another and another.

Every morning we counted the survivors, and hoped they would loosen their hold before dark, and let us sleep.

At last Papazi began his work, most of which I missed watching. There were parboilings to get the emaciated little creatures from their shells, and individual operations to remove their less delectable portions. There were endless scrubbings of each lovely shell, with little curved brushes made especially in Paris. Then the cadavers were tucked into their coffins again, and Papazi and Madame Rigoulot made an extra trip to market for the parsley, the garlic, and the sweet butter.

The last scene I caught through the dining-room door: Plume and Doudouce bent gravely over a lighted table, pouring the hot sauce into each up-ended snail shell. Their hands trembled very slightly, and Plume's hot tongue stuck out.

And when we finally ate them, *les escargots d'or,* sizzling hot and delicately pungent on our little curved forks, it was clear that "store snails" were only for those unhappy people who did not live with Papazi—or those fools too impatient to wait for his slow perfection.

The best days there with the Rigoulots were Sundays. Then Papazi, an apron over his pinstriped trousers and his skullcap set somewhat more jauntily than usual on his smooth pink head, made a tart for the grandchildren.

On feast days, on the innumerable birthdays, he worked alone in the kitchen. He created now a *diplomate au kirsch,* now a *bombe Nesselrode* or a dozen *coupes Dame Blanche.* He worked in a controlled frenzy, if such there be: His moustache, when we peeked silently at him through the one dim window into the courtyard, vibrated like a small, pale crescent moon above his tight mouth, and his little fat hands flicked aspishly, with delicate dead reckoning, from the bowls to the bottles to the jars and back again.

It would have been impudence raised to the celestial degree to interrupt him then. He was inviolate, a Jehovah *en cuisine.*

Sundays were different. They were really more fun. We could approach him, always with respect, but on that holy day, with a kind of affectionate curiosity. He opened the heavenly doors and for a short time after church allowed us to watch while he threw together something completely simple, he insisted—something we were perhaps capable of understanding and one day even copying.

Papazi had been a Lutheran for fifty years in Alsace, not so much from conviction as from a melodramatic hope that he might have to fight for his "faith," or perhaps be stoned. Now, in Dijon, he stalked through the Sunday streets with an exalted glare on his round old face, praying, I am sure, for a little Catholic persecution.

He never got anything but most respectful nods, of course, from all the other retired pastry- and candy-makers and their wives, but by the time he returned home and tied the Sunday apron over his pinstripes he was in a state of quasi-religious elation.

"Hah," he would mutter above the sound of the symphony coming from Berlin on the radio. "Hah! We Protestants are a small sect here. That I admit. Small but strong! We can fight when provoked! Separate burial grounds! Hah!"

And Plume and Doudouce and I, and the eldest brother Dédé and his roommates down from Saint-Cyr now and then, would huddle in awe in the dark corners of the room, watching Papazi grit his strong teeth (teeth that had lived for almost eighty years in a constant sweet syrup of his own concoctions!) while he tossed together the Sunday Tart.

It was almost always a tart. Occasionally, if the symphonies were too good to be listened to without both his ears, he would wait until about an hour before supper and make some kind of fritters. They were of apples or cherries or cheese, and he piled them like small, dark clouds on the big platter in the center of the supper table, and we ate perhaps a hundred of them and slept deeply and sweetly through the night.

We always liked it a little better, though, when he started to work as soon as Radio Berlin or Prague came on. That would be in the middle of the afternoon. The music would swell and thunder, through the stuffy dining room into the miserable cramped, dark kitchen, and Papazi's nose under his skullcap would shine cheeringly in the glare from the one dangling lightbulb, and his little hands would dart into the making of the Tart.

It was always the same kind. It always looked exactly like the last one. It always tasted like what it was: the most delicious tart in a whole land famous for them.

Papazi made the pastry first, with a nonchalance I've only seen in one other cook, a Black woman named Bea, who threw flour and shortening into a bowl at least three times a week and pulled out the lightest, tenderest soda biscuits ever to be baked and eaten. There was the same airy, almost unconscious concentration about both people, the old, fat *confiseur* in Dijon and the young, smooth, laughing woman in California.

Papazi talked while he mixed and rolled, and then flipped the delicate sheet of dough into the wide, flat baking tin he'd brought with him from Alsace. It was the conventional French shape, with steep, short sides, and about two feet across. He twirled it on his hand and slashed off the hanging dough, and then quickly put it out on the window-ledge to chill, in winter, or in summer tossed it to Doudouce to run proudly with it down into the wine cellar.

And then he, and sometimes Plume if the impish child had not been too monkeylike that week at the *lycée,* would peel apples from Normandy, and cut them into thin, even half-moons, and toss them into a bowl of white wine to keep bright and crisp. When only two more apples were left, and Papazi judged Plume could cope with them, he jumped up, humming and dancing to the music from the radio, and beat eggs and cream and nutmeg into a custard. He flicked an egg white over the chilled pastry with one of his innumerable brushes. He poured the custard in. It filled the shallow pan just half full.

He took the apple slices from the bowl one by one, almost faster than we could see, and shook off the wine and laid them in a great, beautiful whorl, from the outside to the center, as perfect as a snail shell. We said not a word. The music trembled in the room. The light burned down. Papazi shuffled the thin pieces of fruit like a wizard or a little fat god, and they seemed to fall out from his hands and fall rightly into place. He did it as effortlessly as a spider spins a web.

Then he poured thin apricot glaze over the whole, shook it gently, and slid it into the oven. He stood for a second looking at the shut door, and laughed sadly, like any man, either earthly or celestial, after the final pang of creation. We stirred in our dark corners. He looked straight at us, for the first time since the beginning of the pastry.

"You see?" he said. "It is the Tart, the simplest form of *pâtisserie.* I admit it is also one of the most complex. It takes years of careful behavior, like—like being the one Protestant in a nest of papists! It takes *guile!*"

And he flung off his apron, shook it once professionally, and put on his cutaway. We followed him silently into the dining room, to listen to the end of Radio Berlin and wait for the Tart to be baked for our Sunday supper.

The Sunday-noon dinners there in that odorous dark crumbling house were monumental, Gargantuan. We moved from the little room to the big one, the Sunday one, the main salon where Madame Bitsch had lived during our first year there. There was a clean white cloth on the table, and the chairs were wide and leather soft. Red and white wines were at either end of the table, in carafes . . . usually a bottle or two on the sideboard, and one of Papazi's unlabeled liters of *Kirsch d'Alsace* or *Rhum Martinique,* sent him fifty, sixty, seventy years before . . . .

Al and I finally took to sneaking away after the noon meal, as soon as we had partially recovered from it, and going to Crespin for a few oysters, or to any place at all for a salad and a piece of bread.

Sometimes Monsieur Rigoulot would see us, on his way home after an afternoon of café-gambling or other more active gambols, and then there would be red-eyed Monday questions from Madame. It was impossible to tell her that we simply could not eat for a few hours; she did not know people like that.

She herself was one of the most unreservedly sensual people I know of. She was not at all attractive physically. She neglected her person, mainly because she gave every ounce of her time and energy to feeding us. So she was bedraggled and shiny and often smelled. And, what is even more distasteful, she was needlessly ailing. Such a state is repulsive to me. She had really violent monthly headaches which seemed, to my ill-trained eye, pure bilious attacks.

It was almost a Jekyll-and-Hyde thing with her, the change from one hour to the next, once a month. She would to my impatiently young eyes send out little waves of despondency and odorous sweat, and then, like a bomb flash, she would be *there,* in it, swept up, round and round, in pain and duress vile, and untouchability. It was, yes, a biblical ordeal, one for all of us to undergo, but especially my poor fat bilious weary and above all worried friend. For three or four days she would stagger from stove to table and back again, cooking and then eating with the same concentrated fervor as always, while her eyes were almost mad with pressure, and her face was gray.

She connected these *crises de nerfs névralgiques,* as she always called them, in some way with her unhappiness in marriage, and spent a good part of the time convincing her one daughter that taking the veil was much preferable. In spite of my exasperation with her, as I saw her eating with such steady gourmandise at her own rich soups and tarts and stuffings, I knew she suffered like hell and I longed to help her.

She was still a terrible snob, in spite of the cruel way her life had changed from its first spoiled lavish opulence, and would sweep and market all morning and then put on her one good black dress and go to a concert, where she sat in the stiff position taught her in school in Germany and listened to music which her poor tired ears could never hear. She saw to it that somehow her children went to the correct piano teachers and the best schools, not because she wanted them to be well educated but because she was proud in the face of her own steady social decline, and knew that she was better than any of the plump matrons who now occupied the position she had once taken as her right.

She was a stupid woman, and an aggravating one, and although I did not like her physically I grew to be deeply fond of her and even admiring of her. For years we wrote long and affectionate letters, and on the few times I returned to Dijon we fell into each other's arms ... and then within a few minutes I would be upset and secretly angry at her dullness, her insane pretenses, and all her courage and her loyal blind love would be forgotten until I was away from her again. . . .

Long after the Second World War I got a letter from her at last. It had been more than ten years, which to me seemed like a thousand and, since I could guess what had happened to her since our last interchange of gushing amicability, had been around ten thousand to her there where she was.

I knew she had fled at the first invasion. From then on, for about three years, I tried to reach her through the Red Cross, unsuccessfully. I loved her, and grieved.

All the time until her letter came—since our last strained "five-o'clock" in a fifteen-century town house, shabby, smelling of rats—I had felt her heavy in my heart. The weight was gastronomical, the way that, at times, it can be more of a tragicomical or purely sexual kind.

Once during World War II Genêt in *The New Yorker* wrote matter-of-factly of a recipe for stewed guinea pig, newly sent her from a good cook in the provinces. I saw my dear friend, fat, almost blind with stubborn myopia, the curls that had once been pretty stringing down over the pouchy cheeks that had once been beautiful, desired; I saw her killing the little rodent, cleaning it, cooking it artfully with the dregs of a hoarded wine bottle, and I saw her serving it, and she flushed and happy, to anyone at all who would know what she had done for this moment, but especially me, so removed by time, space, and the sound of bombs.

Her letter moved me, in an almost shocking way. It was banal, for how could it be anything else? Had we ever been anything but dull with one another? Had we ever, one to the other, put out our spirits' fingertips and touched the sensitive fronds, the tendrils, the antennae of what each human is condemned to be, a fern, a vine, a slow sea creature?

Yes. Yes, I said passionately, we often had. Surely she must have understood my anguished shyness, when I was a young bride and she mother of three big children, and weary wife. She must have known, I said, how deeply I often felt her weariness, her loyal wifedom, and above all her motherhood, when I had none of such things and was an eager lover, no more. I used to walk through the courtyard past the kitchen, slim and fresh and flagrantly untried, and call out happily to her and be pleased at her smile and the way she pushed back her steamy locks from her forehead. I never saw myself, for I was still too young to have inside eyes open, in her place there over the pots and ramekins.

Now I do. Now I know what she must at times have felt, as she looked through the vapors at my nonchalant head, and then later sat tiredly behind the tureen on the spotted cloth, ladling out the finest broths, the subtlest brews indeed, that I have ever eaten. Now I know the mockery she kept so decently hidden, the time she offered to teach me what she knew about cookery and I thanked her and said no. My God, how could I have been so stupid? I cringe and shiver, to think of sitting there in the stuffy clumsy little room and saying it, and of her good accepting smile, her continued benevolence, to me, great Saxon inept lout that I was.

In many ways I was a fool not to accept her offer. But I knew that she would drive me crazy, shatter all my carefully educated reserve and self-control, so that I might scream at her or hit her with a spoon. Instead, I said that my university work took all of my time.

She was the best unprofessional cook I have ever known, and in spite of my toplofty renegation of her services I learned a great deal from her, in a kind of unconscious and therefore perhaps doubly potent osmosis of my gastronomical self. I soaked her up.

We used to talk a lot about marriage. I was interested in hers, because after almost twenty years it was so obviously a bad one. She admitted that herself, and in the insidious way of good women she managed beautifully to make the three children hate their father for her battered sake. She had been married, thanks to her dowry, to a promising young automobile inventor, and then spent the rest of her life watching him laugh and wink his way through all the money and a hundred careless jobs, until at last he was a garage mechanic and she was a penniless slave; and still she believed passionately that the provincial French system of marriage was the only successful one. I, on the other hand, argued as fervently for the American way of encouraging young people physically attracted to one another to marry in spite of a complete lack of parental and financial blessings.

Madame and I got divorces in the same year, and exchanged somewhat woebegone letters on the subject. Hers were full of a kind of courage I shall probably never have, and were written by a mind perhaps ten or eleven years old.

Monsieur Rigoulot could not stand facing life, so with his big moustache and bright red face he went off with his mistress and became a poacher. Madame Rigoulot went into widow weeds and heavy bitterness. She was divorced, and that made her a divorcee, which was terrible in the Church.

After the divorce she left Dijon, where she had struggled so miserably against poverty and the town's pity, and went with Papazi and the two younger children nearer their dear Alsace. Then she was evacuated. . . .

Monsieur Rigoulot was a coarse kindhearted man, who in this country would belong to the American Legion and any local clubs that had good times. In Dijon he lived mostly in the cafés, playing cards and talking about the happy war days, when he had been a captain and had a mistress who later became a famous movie star. He had also won a few decorations, but they were not important to him compared with *la belle Arlette* or whatever her name was.

He drank a lot, especially if he knew that Madame had one of her headaches or there were an unusual lot of bills to be paid. He was always polite, and even gay, with us, although sometimes he used to snarl at the children. Papazi he feared and respected, and borrowed money from, as if the old man had supported him for so long that it was only logical to continue. Papazi was equally polite, and as soon as Dédé was twenty-one paid for a divorce. He despised his son-in-law.

The children did too, in that insidious way of young things . . . never openly mocking, but always a little too meek, too indomitably servile.

André, always known as Dédé, was the oldest and the only one who ever called his mother *la pigeonne,* from *La P'tit Jeanne.* Dédé was a surly oafish boy, with thick outlines and small eyes like his father's. They quarreled bitterly and often at the dinner table. He openly hated the way his mother had to work, and was the only one of the family who ever seemed to resent our presence. His table manners were dreadful, and I resented him even more than he did me, probably.

He studied with a kind of dogged hopelessness for Saint-Cyr, and finally got in, the last name on the list. His mother wrote of his marriage . . . much beneath him, she managed to imply. And when France fell he was a captain in the *Pompiers de Paris,* and had a "pretty eight-room apartment near his garrison where Simone awaits the first-born son," Madame wrote in her fine overcrossed lines of purple ink. So much for Dédé. He was a boor, in spite of his fine palate.

Jean-Jacques or Plume, as he was always called, was another

thing entirely. He was the most like an elf of any person I have known, and also like a monkey, with the same bright inhuman gaze. He was about fourteen when we knew him. He refused to go to school, so in turn Papazi bribed every reputable candy maker in Dijon to make him as an apprentice. He made all the workers laugh so hard they ruined the bonbons and the tarts, and the bosses shivered in their beds with worry over his next trick. Would Plume decorate the wedding cake of a maiden trying to hide her Semite origins with a Star of David made of rosebuds? Would he put oil instead of Cointreau in the little chocolate bottles for the Bishop's Christmas party?

Plume, in spite of Papazi's renown, was forced to conclude that he would like to be a piano tuner, a watchmaker, a lawyer, and a dancing master. Nothing perturbed him, and he flitted like a gentle grinning little satyr through the offices and factories and streets of Dijon.

We used to see him sometimes coming out of the most expensive brothels, always with the same mischievous detachment in his small face, and some of the prostitutes told Al that he was a great favorite among them, so tender and courteous and charming. He was that way at home too, and we all loved him.

After we left he got a job with the automobile factory where his father had once been well known, and suddenly, perhaps because of the divorce, his fey attitude clarified and he became almost a wizard with engines. He went to Algiers. His mother wrote happily about him. He was invalided home once while I was in France, and I saw him for a minute, shaking with fever. He bent over my hand. I still felt as if he were fourteen, not in his twenties, and could hardly keep from smiling. I felt his kiss on my skin for a long time.

Then, in the first criminal hysteria of mobilization in France, he was snatched from the auto works where by now he was a prized technician, and put to digging trenches. Within a few days he died of pneumonia.

"When you watch the dirt being shoveled onto your son's coffin," his mother wrote to me in her precise flowing hand, "you have an almost uncontrollable desire to throw back your head and howl like a wounded beast."

And Doudouce? Her name was France, because she was born

on the first Armistice Day. She was a serious little girl, short and round, with worry in her eyes, and her mother's sensual mouth. Even when we knew her, starting her teens, she worked heavily and earnestly at her lessons. She was already resolved never to marry, never to subject herself to the monthly headaches and the daily labor that she saw in her mother, and she had decided for herself that being a teacher was better than being a nun. We used to try to make her seem more like a little girl, but it was not until after we left, after the divorce, that Plume taught her gaiety. Doudouce kept on with her studying, but she danced too.

She passed her examinations. Then, to her mother's proud bewilderment, she went all alone to Paris, studied medicine, and became a roentgenologist. She was there when the city fell, and I wonder now whether Papazi's fanatical hatred of the Boches upheld her, or whether the latent sensuality in her small round body taught her that headaches are not always made by men, even German men.

I think often of her, and of Plume so quickly out of it, and of my poor stupid friend their mother, and the pouting Dédé. I remember with a kind of anguish the prodigal bounty of their table, and their childlike inability to conceive of anything but richness and warmth and sensory perfection for themselves and their friends. They were less able than ordinary people to withstand the rigors of physical hunger.

I think of them as I used to see them, the three children bending over the steaming stove, their eyes intent and beautiful, their ears listening reverently to Papazi as he waved a spoon and told them the history of the *sauce Soubise* or the carp dumplings he concocted, while Madame sat for a few stolen moments at the dining-room table, account books spread before her straining eyes but a little plate of *truffes au chocolat* beside her one free hand, or a small glass of *anisette*. . . .

That is why I thought more of them, probably, than of any other of my tortured, burned, starved, dead, and dying friends during World War II. That is why, when I read about the stew of guinea pigs, I wept inside, not for the conditioned repulsiveness of it but for my friend's pride in being able to make it a quondam masterpiece.

She was the most insanely extravagant woman I have ever

known in a comparatively short but extravagant life. Every day of the many months that I ate at her table and lived under her mortgaged roof, I felt this almost deliberate madness of spending in her. Once she asked me, and I knew it was after much nerve-steeling on her part, if we could increase our monthly payments by even a dollar or so. I pull back, for many reasons, at remembering the scene: the two of us in the tiny room, two tiny glasses of plum brandy before us, our tiny minds nibbling like newborn mice at our late-born caution in the face of the way we both lived, she in a kind of flood of rich sauces and fine wines, I in my own newly discovered sensuality. We drank and looked and drank . . . and finally I said, in the first such decision of my too-sheltered life, that I would pay her extra secretly but would not bother my husband about it, and she smiled in an exhausted way, confused and upset by having had to speak of the cost of things, and that night she opened a bottle of distilled wild strawberries that her father had gathered, fifty years before, when he was apprenticed to a caterer in Alsace. It stuck in my throat at first, and then in the flush of my friend's warm unquestioning generosity, I drank to her, to myself, to the world. I had been humbled, never to be so proud again, but it had been done like a mercy killing, instinctively and with love.

It seems plain by now that part of my love for her is guilty. That does not worry me. I wish very much that I could have taken her offers and learned all she had to teach, and in the same way that I could have given her some physical aid and lessened her heavy load. Neither thing happened. Instead she went on, day by day and meal by meal, turning out such feathery crusts, such almost dangerously light fritters, such omelets and ragouts and tarts, as I have not seen before or since.

I have a few of her recipes (she wrote them laboriously, late at night, and there are grease smudges on the papers, and I accepted them nonchalantly, perhaps as my due, although God knows for what), and although I can barely decipher their elaborate scrolling and much less follow their grams-and-liters, they evoke for me an elegance of gastronomical thought that is untouchable. This woman, poor wracked harried creature, never faltered in the way she nurtured us. No matter what her monetary anguish, she never used false butter, nor bruised peaches, nor cut wine. Nor did she lie to us. . . .

Perhaps Papazi was luckiest. "You will be saddened, my dear," Madame wrote a few months before war started, ''that our beloved Papazi is no more. His end was one you will appreciate, as the good God's special reward to such a devout and faithful servant of Epicurus.

"Lately my poor father has forgotten his many financial misfortunes, and our table has been worthy indeed of the greatest *confiseur-pâtissier* of Alsace, past, present, and future. Wednesday noon, in honor of Plume's new position at the factory, Papazi prepared with his own hands and very little help from me a repast such as we have not seen for years. We began, as a compliment to me, with my own recipe for *Potage Richelieu* (Bring 200 grams of the finest butter to the bubble, add . . . but I shall write it on another sheet of paper, my dear . . .), and then had snails, which Plume and Doudouce and I gathered ten days ago in the woods, just as in the old days . . . do you remember the many times we starved them in the courtyard, and you helped us wash the shells with Papazi's little brushes?. . . and after a small but delicious *soufflé* of Gruyère to refresh our palates, we ate a tongue with *sauce Philippe,* which recipe I shall also enclose in case you do not remember it.

"I do not wish to weary you, my very dear friend. Suffice it to say that at the end there was to be a *Diplomate au Kirsch d'Alsace,* made just as always with the marinated fruits. With that, having opened almost the last of our best bottles for the first part of the repast, I planned to serve coffee in the Algerian way to please Plume, rather than champagne as we used to do it in Dijon.

"But just before we reached that course, our dear Papazi . . . this is painful, as you will understand . . . our dear Papazi, who had been gay and young all day, suddenly stood up, emptied his glass, and then sat down again with a strange smile on his face. His stomach gave out a loud rumble, and he was gone from us."

CHAPTER
TWELVE

M Y MOTHER believed thoroughly that husbands and wives should be separated for long vacations away from each other. And I, as her first born and perhaps most dutiful of all her children, obeyed her dicta without any thought, for a surprising number of years. I still wonder at the wisdom of them and resent the hurt they caused me, as well as my silence always about them.

It did not occur to me to protest when I found that it was all arranged for me to spend my first married summer in England and Ireland with Mother and my next younger sister Anne. And I went along without anything but a secret hurt at the apparent pleasure my young husband showed when he gave me the tickets for the English jaunt.

As it turned out, the summer was aborted by an accident to my mother's knee the first night we were in London, and we came down to Dijon early instead of being trotted through the Irish countryside by the Yankee girl who had been a shy visitor at the turn of the century.

The summer was a good one as I now see it, and it cemented the fine feeling Al and my mother always had for one another. And I never mentioned how hurt I was.

The second summer, though, was harder in every way. But it was worth all my secret pain at the even more obvious pleasure Al expressed so straightforwardly to me when he put me on a slow boat back to California. It seemed like a real deception to me, but once more I played along, the dutiful daughter always, and for the second time around the equally dutiful wife. This time I knew that Al wanted me to leave, and I was also convinced that I was being summoned home for a definite reason, which was left unmentioned until a few days before I was to return to Dijon. The reason was that my sister Norah was to return with me.

Of course, I was really pleased. I had known her since her conception almost, literally, and she was and still remains one of the most important people in my life. There were many things about her living with us that seemed insoluble, so I simply went along once more as the dutiful daughter, and I started back with Norah to rejoin Al in Dijon for my third year.

I knew that we could no longer be students, but instead I would be in charge of a thirteen-year-old child some six feet tall—a proud and beautiful woman who was already in love with her headmaster, and who was obviously unfit in every possible way to enter high school in the town of Whittier. She had been in boarding school for two years, and I knew that my mother had been unable to cope with her after my marriage, and had simply taken to her bed and confided the care of Norah and my younger brother David to a dreamy young school master who ran a small boarding school, and then a summer camp in the nearby hills of Laguna Beach and Glendora. It was all very convenient, and I was the next logical step for Norah. My life with Al had been thoroughly observed by Mother the summer before, during the long weeks she had spent with my sister Anne at the Hôtel Central in Dijon. And so it was the most natural thing in the world for me to find myself returning to my life with Al in the company of my younger sister.

My astonishment was so great that I discussed it with nobody, especially since Al already seemed much more *au courant* than I, as indeed he was. I can say this now without any false sense of accusation, but at the time I was secretly bitter at his having known about the plans for Norah's return before I took off alone for the long trip back to California. An I am sure that neither he nor Mother could have guessed the importance of the months we spent together.

By now it is much too late to ask Al Fisher what he thought

about the strange plan and its possible results, and of course they were never mentioned by Mother. In fact, Norah and Larry Powell are the only ones left who could possibly remember that summer and the year that followed it, and I doubt very much that I ever do ask Norah what she felt. This seems strange to me now, because we were all strong people, but we did as Mother had planned without any questions asked or ever answered. So . . .

There I was in Dijon with this beautiful child and no place to put her. I think she slept on our couch in the purple workroom for a few nights, and she and I walked everywhere about the town. I was aware of her beauty and of her strange clothes, for she was dressed like a child, which she still was in her mother's eyes. I changed her wardrobe into something less juvenile and got her new shoes that were more adapted to the cobbled streets of the old French town. And I did not let her know that she was a sight that struck wonder whenever she walked along the streets.

I remember turning around several times on the rue de la Liberté and seeing people come out of their shops and gaze after her as she sailed along, looking almost seven feet tall in the bright red fez with the long black tassel that she had bought in Paris at the Colonial Exposition on our way from the boat and down to Dijon.

In the next few days we went at our own pace to places I wanted to show Norah. We got lost in the attics of the Palace, looking at armor and tombs and out the windows at the tiled roofs. We looked in windows full of mustard, bought candles in the dim echoing churches, and speared hot snails firmly on our forks.

I showed Norah the tiny owl carved on a stone in the backside of the Church of Notre Dame, and I showed her that she could rub its smooth breast as everybody who knows about it is supposed to do. I forget why, but it has never mattered: The owl itself, so small and ageless, is satisfying enough.

Norah at thirteen was very fond of the tea shops, with a fine capacity for *babas au rhum* at 4:30 in the afternoon. Michelin was the bigger and duller and more prosperous. Duthu, down the rue de la Liberté, made chocolate truffles, and the elegant ladies who sold them picked them up in silver tongs and slipped them into little gilded paper cones tied with gold thread, also very elegant.

THAT AUTUMN was when I decided that I could no longer stand to live as a boarder, which we had done for the past two years. It was plain that the time had come for Al and me to live by ourselves.

For two years we had come twice or three times each day to the small stuffy room on the rue du Petit-Potet with its brown walls, its *"Souvenir de Verdun,"* and its two heads of young deer. For too many months we had forced politeness, interest, enjoyment, to cover the dull and sometimes the ferocious irritation we had felt. We had listened without a twitching muscle to hundreds of bowls of hot soup, dozens of feathery omelets, thousands of glasses of watery *vin ordinaire,* go down the noisy gullets of the Ollangniers and their pensionnaires, and then the Rigoulots. We had learned much from them and accepted a thousand courtesies. They were our friends, patient with our French, interested in our work, amused by our strange ideas, and we loved them. But now, suddenly, they were intolerable, they and their sad quarrels and their gay generosities. And we left, soon after I came back from California, as if we were fleeing the black pox.

I combined showing the town to Norah with looking for a place to put her and another place to put ourselves, as it became increasingly clear that we should not live together. Our needs were too different. Al was finishing up his thesis and spent most of his days at the café writing on it and on his "Ghost in the Underblows." And at night we went always to movies. Norah, in spite of her great height and her obvious maturity, as well as her childlike undeveloped side, was not ready for that kind of student life. And she was too young to live alone at the Rigoulots.

Even after so long in an army town, I still could not always tell a *"gros numéro"* from a reputable house, and managed to interrupt several business transactions and even exchange a few embarrassed salutations with unbuttoned university friends before I found the little apartment we were to live in.

I got Norah into the convent school of Notre Dame des Anges, up the rue Victor Hugo, almost outside of town.

It was a very nice one, but it seemed to me to be terrible for Nonie, even though she did learn to speak some French. The only other person who spoke English at all was an Irish girl who actually spoke nothing but Gaelic. She could at least speak Irish-English when she had to.

It was completely different for Norah. She was so *alone*. And it was hard for her because she only got out on Thursday afternoons and all day Sunday. But I never asked her.

As soon as Norah was safely ensconced at Notre Dame des Anges, we moved into our new apartment. It was in a "low quarter," a blue-collar quarter, and people were embarrassed when we told them. The tram ran past it, and it looked down on a small shabby square that once had held a guillotine, shaded by thick plantain trees around the usual fountain.

Indeed, the quarter was so low that several Dijonnais who had been friendly with us stopped seeing us altogether. What had been an amusing social pastime in the fairly dull town life, coming to tea with us on the rue du Petit-Potet, safely surrounded as we were there by mayors and bishops and the smell of thirteenth-century cellars, became an impossibility when it meant walking through streets that were obviously inhabited by nothing but artisans and laborers. We basked in the new freedom, and absorbed sounds and vapors never met in a politer life.

Our apartment was two floors above a pastry shop, Au Fin Gourmet, and was very clean and airy, with a nice smell. The smell was what made me decide to take it, after days of backing confusedly out of brothels and looking at rooms dark and noisome and as lewdly suggestive as the old crones who showed them to me.

We signed several official certificates, bending over peach tarts and a row of soggy *babas* to reach the ink bottle. The proprietor looked at our signatures, and asked, "Married?"

"Yes," Al said, raising one eyebrow almost invisibly in a way that meant, in those days at least, that in spite of his politely innocent manner his words carried a tremendous reprimand or correction or general social commentary. "Yes. You see we have the same name, and I have marked us as Monsieur and Madame."

"Well," the man said, "it is less than nothing to me, you understand. But the police must be satisfied." He looked amicably at us, wiped his hands again on his sugary apron, and marked out Madame and my profession as student. In place of it he wrote, "Monsieur Fisher, and woman."

His wife, a snappish-looking small person with pink hair and eyebrows and tight mouth, gave us our keys and warned us again that the chambers were now in perfect condition and were expected to remain that way, and we went up the stairs to our own private home for the first time in our lives.

There was a big room with a shiny but uneven tiled floor and two wide windows looking down on the dusty little square. The bed, half-in, half-out a little alcove, did not keep everything from looking spacious and pleasant, especially when we pushed the round table into the corner by the window, and put books on the fake mantlepiece under the wavy old mirror and above the minute woodburning stove. There was a kind of cupboard, which Madame the owner had called *"la chambre noire";* we got some candles for it and turned one of our trunk tops into a washstand, and it was very matter-of-fact in spite of its melodramatic name. Downstairs and toward the back of the courtyard at the end of the long gallery was a public toilet that served all the people on the block. It was an open latrine with three holes, and it was the most exposed one in my European experience.

Outside our front door, on the landing, was a little faucet, where we got water for washing and cooking. It was a chore to carry it, and even more of one to empty the pail from the Black Chamber and the dishwater and what I washed vegetables in, but it was something so new that I did not much mind it. There was a fountain in the square, of course, and I soon learned to take my lettuces and such down there and let the spout run over them, like the other women in the quarter.

The kitchen was astonishing to me, because I had never lived in a place like New York, where, I've heard, people cook on stoves hidden in the bureau drawers. It was perhaps five feet long, and certainly not more than three feet wide. Its floor of uneven baked tiles was scoured to a mellow pinkness. There were two weak shelves, slanting toward the floor. A two-burner gas plate on a tottering wooden table was the stove. To stand at it I had to keep the door open into the other room, but that was all right: The door had been stuck open for several decades.

I made very good things to eat in that kitchen, and I have always felt that this was partly so because one end of it, from side to side and from ceiling almost to floor, was a window. It was a sparkling window of many-paned glass, a window curtained briefly with two silly little dabs of cheap net, a window split down the middle ready to fling open as wide as those windows can be flung, wider really than any other.

It looked over twisted chimney pots to the skies of the Côte d'Or and down through treetops into the square where gibbets and then a guillotine once stood, where wandering circus families set up their gas flares for a night or two by the busy fountain and the *pissoir,* where people moved and talked incessantly above the high wail of a café phonograph playing ten thousand times the record of Josephine Baker's *"J'ai Deux Amours."*

All the noises flowed in and out the window of the tiny kitchen, gay and somber and mysterious and always real, and I may be too sentimental in thinking that they helped me cook some good dishes—but I doubt it.

Of course, we celebrated the first night in the new place, and dined well and late at the Three Pheasants, so that in the morning it was fun to lie in our niched bed and listen to the new noises. We were very sleepy, but we never had heard so much noise, such energetic, lusty, bustling, and stirring noise. We lay for a time and listened.

First we heard the workers in their hard shoes, then the luckier ones with bicycles, and all the bells ringing; the shop shutters being unhooked and folded back by sleepy apprentices; a great beating of pillows and mattresses, so that now and then brown feathers floated past our windows; and always the clanging of the little trams going up into the center of things. Two floors below, we could hear the ocher-painted shutters of our cake shop being lifted clumsily off their hooks. That must be the great stupid girl who had peered through the curtain from the back room yesterday when we signed the papers. We heard her padding heavily along the downstairs corridor that led, we supposed, into the den where cakes were born.

That first morning there was something more, something we were to hear every Wednesday and Saturday, a kind of whispering pattering rush of women's feet, all pointed one way. I should have listened harder and learned.

When we finally got up, we went to the little café with the dark-green front, two doors up from the Fin Gourmet and on one corner of the square, and sat in the sun with *café au lait* and *croissants* still warm from the oven. People peered at us. Who are these tall strangers? What are they doing in our quarter? Not tourists, certainly—but not workers. We could feel curiosity like a mist about us. But the sun was warm, and we watched things on the street.

We saw that the soft rushing came from hundreds of women, all hurrying silently, all dressed in black and carrying ugly black patent-leather or string bags or pushing little carts and empty baby buggies. And while we were sitting there in the sun, two easygoing foreigners, some of the women started coming back against the stream.

Their bags and carts were heavy now, so that the hands that held and pushed them were puffed and red. I saw the crooked curls of green beans and squashes, the bruised outer leaves of lettuces, stiff yellow chicken legs . . . and I saw that the women were tired but full of a kind of peace, too.

Finally Al and I knew what was happening that morning, why we had heard little wheels pushing up toward the center of things, toward *les Halles,* why women had been so busy, where they had gone, why they came homeward now with bent shoulders on the trams and along the streets. Food. Food for their men and their families. And now I had a shelf—two shelves—and a stove, and meals to make for my husband. When I stood up and walked away, saying in English that I would see Al in the apartment at noon, I could feel a gust of curiosity blow after me from the café.

It was almost noon, and too late now to go to the market. I planned innocently to pick up enough food at local stores to last until the next regular market day. The day before, I had bought two aluminum pans and a big spoon and two knives, one little and one big. But today I went half a block away from our café and in the direction of the apartment and stood for a long time looking at the clay casseroles and pots and kettles piled in front of a sunken shop, almost a cellar, near the back of St. Jean's Church.

The first week I tried to feed us was almost too difficult. I learned a hundred things, all the hard way: how to keep butter without ice, how to have good salads every day when they could only be bought twice a week and there was no place to keep them cool (no place to keep them at all, really), how to buy milk and eggs and cheeses and when and where. I learned that *les Halles* were literally the only place to get fresh vegetables and that two heads of cauliflower and a kilo of potatoes and some endives weighed about forty pounds after I'd spent half an hour walking to market and an hour there and missed three crowded trams going home again.

I learned that you bought meat and hard cheese and such by the kilo, but that butter and grated cheese, no matter how much you wanted, were always measured in grams. I learned that the stall-keepers in the market were tough loud-mouthed people who loved to mock you and collect a little crowd, and that they were very friendly and kind too, if you did not mind their teasing.

I learned always to take my own supply of old newspapers for wrapping things, and my own bowls and cans for cream and milk and such. I learned, with the tiredest feet of my life, that feeding people in a town like Dijon meant walking endless cobbled miles from one little shop to another . . . butter here, sausage there, bananas someplace again, and rice and sugar and coffee in still other places.

It was the longest, most discouraging, most exciting and satisfying week I could remember, and I look back on it now with an envy that is no less real for being nostalgic. I do not think I could or would ever do it again; I am too old. But then, in the town I loved and with the man I loved, it was fine.

We ate well, too. It was the first real day-to-day meal-after-meal cooking I had ever done, and it was only a little less complicated than performing an appendectomy on a life raft, but after I got used to hauling water and putting together three courses on a table the size of a bandanna, and lighting the portable stove without blowing myself clear into the living room instead of only halfway, it was fun.

We bought four plates and four forks, instead of two, so that we could entertain! Several of the people we knew found it impossible to condone our new address even with the words "whimsical" and "utterly mad," and very conveniently arranged to meet us in restaurants when they wanted to see us. The faithful ones who picked their way through the crowded streets and up our immaculately clean tenement steps were few, and they were welcome.

I wanted to invite the Rigoulots, but even if we could have asked them to bring their own plates and forks, I did not think the little stove would be able to cook anything they would honestly or even politely call a meal. And by then I was already beginning to have theories about what and how I would serve in my home.

I was beginning to believe, timidly I admit, that no matter how much I respected my friends' gastronomic prejudices, I had at least an equal right to indulge my own in my own kitchen. (I am no longer timid, but not always adamant, when it is a question of religion or old age or illness.)

I was beginning to believe that it is foolish and perhaps pretentious and often boring, as well as damnably expensive, to make a meal of four or six courses just because the guests who are to eat it have always been used to that many. Let them try eating two or three things, I said, so plentiful and so interesting and so well cooked that they will be satisfied. And if they are not satisfied, let them stay away from our table, and our leisurely comfortable friendship at the table.

I talked like that, and it worried Al a little, because he had been raised in a minister's family and had been taught that the most courteous way to treat guests was to make them feel as if they were in their own homes. I, to his well-controlled embarrassment, was beginning to feel quite sure that one of the best things I could do for nine-tenths of the people I knew was to give them something that would make them forget Home and all it stood for, for a few blessed moments at least.

I learned to make *ratatouille* from a large strong woman, a refugee, not political but economic, from an island off Spain: There was not enough food to go around in her family, and she and her husband were the sturdies, so they got out. They ran a vegetable store with one little window and almost no space, and for the fresh stuff she would pop open a trapdoor and somehow get through it down a steep ladder, nimble as a ballet dancer, and bring up cool cabbages or lettuces which they had bought before dawn at the Big Market.

She was a great big beautiful woman: coal-black hair, big black eyes, but a very big, grossly overweight body. I do not know how she squeezed through that little square hole. She and her tiny husband evidently slept, ate, lived down there.

She taught me more than her stew, without knowing that I often pondered on how she washed her gleaming hair and stayed generally so sweet smelling, when it was plain that both she and the lettuces must bathe at the public pump and sleep in the dark cellar or under the little counter. She cooked on a gas ring behind a curtain at the back of the store, and that is how I first came to ask her questions, because her stew had such a fine smell. She looked at me as if I were almost as ignorant as I was, and after my first lesson from her I bought a big earthenware pot, which I still use.

The ingredients were and still are eggplant unpeeled, and onions, garlic, green peppers, red peppers (if they are procurable), plenty of ripe peeled tomatoes, and some good olive oil. Proportions are impossible to fix firmly, since everything changes in size and flavor, but perhaps there should be three parts of eggplant (and/or squash) to two of tomatoes and one each of the peppers and the onions and garlic. I really cannot say.

Everything is sliced, cubed, chopped, minced, and, except for the tomatoes, is put into the pot . . . thrown in, that is, for the rough treatment pushes down the mass. At the end, when there is less than no room, the tomatoes are cubed or sliced generously across the top, and the lid is pressed down ruthlessly. When it is taken off, a generous amount of olive oil must be trickled over the whole, to seep down. Then the lid is put on again. It may not quite fit, but it will soon drop into place. The whole goes into a gentle (300°) oven for about as long as one wishes to leave it there, like five or six hours. It should be stirred up from the bottom with a long spoon every couple of hours. It will be very soupy for a time, and then is when it makes a delicious nourishing meal served generously over slices of toasted French bread, with plenty of grated dry cheese. Gradually it becomes more solid, as the air fills with rich waftings which make neighbors sniff and smile. When it reaches the right texture to be eaten as one wishes, even with a fork, the lid can stay off and fresh shelled shrimps be laid amply on the top, to turn white before they are stirred in . . . or small sausages already cooked well in beer or wine. Or it can simply be left in a turned-off oven, to be chilled later for probably the best so-called *ratatouille* ever eaten.

T HE PEOPLE who came oftenest to our room above the Fin Gourmet were Norah, on her free Thursday afternoons and Sundays away from the convent, and the American student Lawrence, who was like our brother. They were both simple people, and reassuring.

We went to the Foire Gastronomique de Dijon, on one of Norah's Sundays in November, at the place Wilson, a wide avenue that became a big circle or *carrefour,* with a fountain in the middle. Long tents ran from just below the place Wilson down toward the park, where a kind of fair was set up, with circus acts and little rickety Ferris wheels. Music from the carousels blared everywhere at once, and the stands sold glasses of foaming *mousseux* for about a dime, and by the time you got to the end of the tent you felt high and happy or perhaps a little sick. Wine merchants and nougat makers and vendors of elastic supporters crowded side by side down the long grubby flapping aisles. It was noisy and inexpert and fun. We drank a few samples of wine, of course, and got a little bit tipsy but happily so, and Norah, poor Norah, caught swine pox, which is like chicken pox only nastier. She got it from drinking a glass of wine or something, but we had fun for one day there at the fair.

Norah was quite sick and was isolated in the convent for some time after our day at the Foire. Of course, I went up to see her every day, and that was when I gave her books to read by Colette. At the time, Colette was on the "index," and Nonie kept the books under her mattress . . . the only place to keep *anything.* She was "hiding them," and when they found out about it, I had to promise the Mother Superior that she would never read any Colette again. (All the girls there had to bathe under a sheet so that God would not see them naked.)

I had thought Norah would learn good French from reading Colette. I thought Colette wrote very good colloquial French, but I was asked not to come back to the convent to see Norah.

Norah learned early on to cope with too much sherry in the afternoons. Thursday afternoons, she spent partly with me and partly with Madame Porteau who unwittingly educated her on how to hold her liquor well. It was a strange education for a fourteen-year-old American girl.

When Norah came to our rooms I would get a pitcher of milk and a pot of honey. I would put them with a pat of sweet butter on the table, and a big square block of the plain kind of Dijon gingerbread that was called *pavé de santé.* There would be late grapes and pears in a big bowl.

Norah and I would sit by the open window, listening to the street sounds and playing Bach and Debussy and Josephine Baker on the tinny portable phonograph. The food was full of enchantment to my sister, after her gray meals in the convent, and she ate with the slow voluptuous concentration of a *dévouée.*

Lawrence was as satisfactory. He came for real meals, of course, and always brought a bottle of red wine, cheap but good. There would be candles on the table, because the one lightbulb in the room was far in the opposite corner, by the bed.

We would have a big salad always, and something I had made in one of the clay casseroles. I invented with gusto, and after the first days of experimenting with stoves, pots, and the markets, I turned out some fine odorous dishes.

Our long stay with the Rigoulots, where Lawrence still lived, had given all of us a lust for simplicity after Madame's heady sauces. As I remember, the thing we all liked best, with the salad and Lawrence's wine, was a casserole of cauliflower, and bread and fruit afterwards. I made it so often that it became as natural as sneezing to me, and I was put off the track completely when I got back to America and found how different it was . . . the manner of doing it, the flavor, everything.

There in Dijon, the cauliflowers were small and very succulent, grown in that ancient soil. I separated the flowerets and dropped them into boiling water for just a few minutes. Then I drained them and put them in a wide shallow casserole, and covered them with heavy cream and a thick sprinkling of freshly grated Gruyère, the nice rubbery kind that didn't come from Switzerland at all, but from the Jura. It was called *râpé* in the market, and was grated while you watched, in a soft cloudy pile, onto your piece of paper.

I put some fresh pepper over the top, and in a way I can't remember now the little tin oven heated the whole thing and melted the cheese and browned it. As soon as that had happened we ate it.

The cream and cheese had come together into a perfect sauce, and the little flowers were tender and fresh. We cleaned our plates with bits of crisp bread crust and drank the wine, and Al and Lawrence planned to write books about Aristotle and Robinson Jeffers and probably themselves, and I planned a few things, too.

As I say, once back in California, after so many of those casseroles, I found I could never make one. The vegetable was watery, and there was no cream thick enough or unpasteurized and fresh. The cheese was dry and oily, not soft and light. I had to make a sauce with flour in it. I could concoct a good dish, still . . . but it was never so *innocent,* so simple . . . and then where was the crisp bread, where the honest wine? And where were our young uncomplicated hungers, too?

Quite often Jean Matrouchot would come at noon.

He never went anywhere at night, and of course at the *lycée* and the university where he taught there were a hundred stories about his licentious nocturnals. The truth was, I think, that the state of his poor popping eyes, which made it almost impossible for him to read large print in daylight, turned nights into a complete blackness which his pride would never let him confess. He was a misanthrope, and like most such men had fifty friends who would have been glad of a chance to walk with him along the dim and crooked streets; but instead, he sat alone in his hideously furnished "bachelor suite" and went about only in daylight.

He ate his meals in the pensionnaires' room at Racouchot's, and when he came to us for lunch he was like a man breathing after being almost too long without air.

"No rich dark-brown gaudy sauces," he would mutter, bending over his plate and sniffing what he could hardly see. "No ancient meats mummified with spices, exhumed and made to walk again like zombies! My God, no dead birds, rotting from their bones, and hiding under a crust five men have spent their lives learning how to put together so my guts will fall apart!"

"Madame," Jean would say, rising gallantly and spilling all the red wine in our glasses, which he did not see, and putting his napkin carefully on top of the salad, which was two feet away and therefore invisible to him, "*chère* Madame, a true victim of gastronomy, a fugitive from the world-famed Three Pheasants, a starved soul released temporarily from the purgatory of *la haute Cuisine Bourguignonne,* salutes you!"

Jean would bow, I would thank him, Al and I would whisk the more obvious damage from the table, and we would sit back to a somewhat heavy but enjoyable noon dinner.

Jean liked potatoes, so there would be a casserole of them fixed in the cauliflower routine, and quite often a watercress salad and steaks broiled somehow on the top of the stove. Then we would eat some good cheese . . . the Brie from the shop across the square was wonderful in that autumn weather, with the hot days, and the chilly nights to keep it from ripening too fast . . . and drink some more wine.

He had been an interpreter for the Americans in the last war, and on his good days he would tell us fantastic stories about the peaceful occupation of Beaune and all the homesick generals who called him Johnny. On his middling days he would tease me masterfully, like a fat Voltaire, for my class translations of "Gilpin's Ride." And on the bad days he would mutter such cynicisms as we had never heard, in French as rich and ripe as the cheese he loved, about the world and his honest hatred of it.

He was a strange passionately cold man, the kind who wants to be disliked and has true friends like us to refute all his intellectual desires. I think often of him, and of the hunger he showed for our food, and of the half-blind way his eyes would watch our faces, as if behind all the smug youthful foolishness he saw something he was looking for.

He was very different from Miss Lyse. She came often to eat with us, too, and I don't think she ever looked once at us. If she did, we were simply a part of all the sixty or so years of people who had fed her. She was charming to us; she sang for her supper, as life had taught her to, and she ate with the same ferocious voracity of any little bird while she kept us entertained.

I don't know how she ate so much at one time. It was the result of years of practice, surely, years of not knowing just when another good meal would come her way. She was like a squirrel, with hidden pouches for the future. Norah and Lawrence and Jean Matrouchot were as spindly ghosts compared with her, and meals big enough for six of us melted to a few crumbs almost before I had the time to serve them. Her manners were good, and she talked constantly in her funny mixture of nursery-English and London-French, and yet the lunch would be liquidated in the time Al and I usually spent on a salad or tart.

I tried sometimes to see if I could stump her; I would make a bowl of two whole kilos of Belgian endive, cut into chunks and mixed with marinated green beans and sweet red peppers and chives. There would be a big casserole of fish and mushrooms and such in cream. I'd buy rich tarts at Michelin's.

Halfway through the meal Al and I would lie back in our chairs, listening and watching in a kind of daze. Miss Lyse was like something in a Disney film . . . nibble bite chew nibble nibble . . . through everything on the table, until it would not have surprised us at all to have her start conversationally, daintily, with a flick of her bright dark eyes and a quirk of her white head, on the plates themselves and then the books, right down the mantelpiece, Shakespeare, Confucius, *Claudine à l'Ecole* . . . *les Croix de Bois, The Methodist Faun* . . . nibble nibble crunch.

"That was so delicious, my dears," she would say at the end, wiping her mouth nicely and getting up with a brisk bob. "You are most kind to an old lady. And now I must thank you and be off. The Countess Malinet de Rinche is in from the country and I am having tea with her. This was *such* a nice little lunch together! Shall we say for the same day next week? Then I can tell you all about the dear Countess! Her sons! *Mon Dieu!"*

And Miss Lyse would give me a dry sweet-smelling peck on both cheeks and be out of the door before we could ever get to our feet.

Would she really have tea with the unknown Countess What's-her-name, whose sons were less interesting than dead sea fruit to us? Would she eat again until we next saw her? Did she really have *sous* enough for bread? We never knew.

It worried me, and I resolved to buy nine caramel tarts, instead of six, for the "little lunch" we knew she would not forget to take with us in exactly a week. . . .

I had one letter from her after the last invasion. It was vigorous and amusing, although by then she must have been almost a hundred years old. She had been evacuated to a wretched little village near Clermont-Ferrand, and she had organized all the children into a band, to be ready to greet the Tommies in their own tongue when they came marching in. She said nothing about herself . . . but I have a belief that as long as there was life in that proud-headed little body, she would find crumbs.

ONE NIGHT about ten o'clock, perhaps a week after Al was awarded his doctorate at the *faculté,* we stopped on our way home from a dinner party and stood looking at each other for a minute in the cold street. It was the night before Christmas, I remember.

Then, without a word, we headed for the station. We bought two tickets for Strasbourg on the midnight train, *that* midnight, not the one a week away when we had planned to go.

Most of our things were ready to be shipped. We asked the station master to have them brought from our apartment in a day or two. And I arranged to come back the next week to get Norah out of the convent and into its sister house in Strasbourg. Then we ran down the back streets to our flat, routed out the saw-faced cake maker who lived just below us in his libelously named shop, Au Fin Gourmet, and arranged in five minutes all such questions of refunds, taxes, rental papers as he would have preferred to spend five hours on. We threw our last few things into a suitcase and I left a hasty note for Norah, to be delivered the next day, saying I would be back in one week for her.

We left the door open on our dear little apartment without one backward glance of regret or even gratitude, and when we were finally sitting in the Buffet de la Gare, drinking a last coffee with a porter who had become our friend in the past years, we breathed again.

We were fleeing. We were refugees from the far-famed Burgundian cuisine. We were sneaking away from a round of dinner parties that, we both calmly felt sure, would kill us before another week was over.

Ever since Al's masterly and amusing public oral defense of his thesis, which drew almost as big a crowd in the *faculté* amphitheater as had the last visit from a footloose Balkan regent, we had been deluged with invitations. Most of them were from lawyers, viscounts, and even professors who, in spite of the obvious cordiality of the *faculté* dean and the rector toward us, had peered suspiciously at us over the tops of their newspapers and waited until now to bestow the accolade of their social recognition.

For almost three years they had watched us, and observed to their cynical amazement that we were breaking every precedent established by former American students: We stayed; we didn't get drunk; Al actually worked hard enough to be awarded a degree, and I actually let other men alone, in spite of wearing the same color lipstick as the upper-bracket broads. And now we were guaranteed safe. Al had earned a right to wear a little round bonnet edged with rabbit fur and I, fortunate among all women, could now look forward to being the wife of a full professor some day, instead of an instructor.

"They really seem charming," people whispered about us in the discreetest drawing rooms of Dijon. "Lunch? A small dinner?"

Suddenly we were like catnip, after all those blessed months of being stinkweed. The closed doors swung open, and we found ourselves drowning in a sea of Burgundy's proudest vintages, Rheims' sparkle, Cognac's fire. Snails, *pâtés, quenelles de brochet;* always a great chilled fish *in toto* on a platter; venison and pheasants in a dozen rich brown odorous baths; intricate ices and well-laced beaten creams . . . and all of them served to the weighty tune of polite conversation, part condescending and part awed: It was too much for us.

The unsuspected strain of getting ready for the doctorate and then this well-meant deluge of hospitable curiosity made us feel that "we must press lettuce leaves upon our brows," or die.

And that is why we were hiding in the buffet, that cold December night. We suddenly felt rested, knowing the train was almost there for us. We would send telegrams . . . I would write letters . . .

Our friend the porter piled us into the compartment. We shook hands. The train shivered for a minute, and then started slowly to pull northward.

AFTERWORD

Any kind of afterword to this book will be considered a refutation of the old saw that with age the immediate past fades and that only the earlier days are clear and strong in one's memory. The truth is that I remember everything in my life with equal clarity and could as easily write about the last time I was in Dijon as I could about the first days there. This calls for some overloading of my emotions now and then, especially since I seem to be outliving many of my compatriots and peers and suchlike.

I feel sure that I could walk down the rue de la Liberté today as easily as I did in 1978 when Norah and I stayed there for a few days, or as I did in 1929. The shops would be different, and the cafés, and there would be a new movie house on the place d'Arcy, but I would have changed more than the street itself.

Of course, Georges Connes and Henriette have died by now, but I continue to feel that their children are part of my family. Georges swore that he would not die until his one son Pierre, the *petit crapaud,* had been given a Nobel Prize as an astrophysicist. And he blandly announced when he was eighty that he would live to be a hundred if necessary. However, he died after a fall down a rocky ledge at the old house he had inherited from his father and mother.

Henriette sat by his bedside for the last few days of his life in Montpellier where he died, and wrote to me as if I were a dear friend. This was surprising to me for I continued always to hold her

157

in shy and almost scared esteem, even though she had spent time twice with me when I was living in Saint Helena in the fifties and sixties. This unexpected warmth grew steadily more overt as time passed and by the time she died in Pierre's home outside of Paris, I felt completely at ease with her. It was very rewarding to me. It proved my point that I am blessed amongst women, for many good reasons but especially because I have friends that last a lifetime, and of course far beyond if I should outlive them.

Pierre, the little toad, will never be a Nobel Prize winner, although he and his wife Janine have long composed a team of married astrophysicists that has been compared with the Curies and their like. He was always a hulking loudish man compared to Georges, although he resembles him more as he grows older. For a long time he was hostile toward me, because I wrote stories that were published about his father and mother and even about his grandfather PéPé. He was very censorious for many years and spoke sneeringly of me to his parents and to my face too, as a person who dared mention the Connes as if they were human. Then suddenly, sometime after Georges's death, he came several times to Saint Helena and in the most friendly fashion. I do not know what changed him but it was surprising to me. By now, I think of him with real affection and I stay in touch with Janine, and through the two of them, their children, Elizabeth and Yves.

The Connes are the only people we never left behind us and by now I feel truly pleased to hear from Larry Powell that Pierre comes almost yearly as far as Arizona, to take long walks in the hills with the strange little man that Larry Powell has become. By now, he is tiny in stature and looks as if he might disappear. He is a very famous man and rightly so, for he has spent his whole life since Dijon with books, and he is world famous as a librarian. I do not see him very often anymore but we will remain staunch friends forever.

Al Fisher's death made me a widow for the third time when he died in the early seventies, and I do not know any other survivors of those first three years in France, except for Larry Powell and Ward Ritchie and my sister Norah. She has always been a part of my life and always will be. She remains as much a stranger to me as when we first walked down the rue de la Liberté, but then perhaps I was not meant to know her anymore than I knew myself then in Dijon. We were always congenial and I do not know how much she realized in 1931 that she had entrusted herself to a ghost. By now we are much the same age, but I still feel awed by her precocious maturity as much as I did when we first stood in front of Notre-Dame and watched the Jacquemart and his wife and two children parade jerkily and monumentally from one side to the other of the great church. I think always of the tiny owl carved with such surprising discretion high up on one of the flying buttresses, and of how Norah could reach it so easily when she was very young.

I remember how surprised I was to hear and understand my first French right there by the old church. I had been in Dijon only a few months and suddenly realized that I was listening to some little street boys without even trying to understand them, who were passing just at noon when the usual small gaggle of tourists and local citizens paused to watch the parade of Jacquemart and his family.

"How hideous they are," the little children cried mockingly, so that no one knew whether they were referring to the iron family, or to the rows of public gargoyles on the façade, or to us common people. *"Qu'ils sont moches,"* they cried jeeringly. *"Moches, moches."*

It was a word I had never heard before but I knew exactly what it meant, which in true gutter style was much stronger than any translation could make it. The word *moche* means much more than merely ugly or sinister or hideous, and I never heard the word again, although once I read about it in a dictionary of French slang, which I was consulting for a translation of the life of Maurice Chevalier. *Moche,* according to the dictionary, is untranslatable really, but it was very clear to me when it floated into my deaf ears the first time.

The last time I saw the jerky old metal figures creaking so tinnily across the façade of Notre-Dame, I heard as clearly as I had some fifty years earlier that word *moches* again, and agreed. It seemed unnecessary to tell Norah about this suddenly very important day in my life, just as it always has. She more than anybody could understand what I mean by that, since she too speaks always with reserve and self-respect of almost any part of our lives together. This is because she is a ghost too, probably.

A Note About the Author

M. F. K. Fisher was born in Albion, Michigan, in 1908, but grew up in Whittier, California. After attending a number of schools in California and Illinois, Mrs. Fisher spent three years in France studying at the University of Dijon. Her first book, *Serve it Forth,* was published in 1937 and established her as a food writer of note, a reputation reinforced by her subsequent books, among them *Map of Another Town, The Gastronomical Me,* and the translation of Brillat-Savarin's *The Physiology of Taste.* She has also won acclaim for *Among Friends,* a memoir of her early life in Whittier, and *As They Were* and *Sister Age,* essays on aging. She has been living in Glen Ellen, California, for the past twenty or so years.

MP8W